Literature as a Mode of Travel

Literature as a Mode of Travel

Five Essays and a Postscript

With an Introduction by Warner G. Rice

New York
The New York Public Library
1 9 6 3

Library of Congress Catalog Card Number: 63–23262

Note: The editor has not attempted to bring the various authors' spellings of "traveller/traveler" &c into uniformity, the two traditions being of about equal force.

Reprinted from the
Bulletin of The New York Public Library
June 1962; March, April, May, June, October 1963
Printed at The New York Public Library

form p719 [xii-13-63 15c]

Table of Contents

Illustrations

Introduction: Travellers and Travel Books

FOUR OF THE FIVE essays reprinted here were originally prepared for sessions of the English Institute held at Columbia University in 1961 and 1962. The fifth, Professor Paul Fussell's account of Patrick Brydone, was, like the rest, first published in the *Bulletin of The New York Public Library*. The series was designed to illustrate ways in which travellers and travel books have extended knowledge, enlarged ideas, served as an index to culture, and contributed to imaginative literature. It is varied enough to suggest that many opportunities lie open for research in this field — a field which is very spacious indeed.

Several travellers' accounts survive from antiquity and the middle ages — e g in histories, as well as in such writings as those of Strabo, Pausanias, or Marco Polo. It was the printing press, however, that made possible the wide dissemination of reports of those voyages which the first great modern age of discoveries produced, and it was the spirit of curiosity engendered by that age which motivated the first professional travellers. From the time of the irrepressible Tom Coryate and the indomitable William Lithgow men (and women) have ventured into far places, "inquisitive after foreign news," and have returned to shape their journals into books which delight and instruct. That these have been well received by readers is attested by the large bibliographies devoted to the subject. The statistics of book production justify the estimate that in the category of Geography and Travel new titles published in English now annually total about one-third the number representing history, and one-fifth the number representing fiction. Certainly the materials which travellers might exploit have proved inexhaustible. In modern times the rapid expansion of communications has encouraged the exploration of every quarter of the globe. A second age of discovery succeeded the first; so, in our own day we have witnessed a third, as explorers have forced the arctic regions to yield up their secrets; and we now can predict a fourth, as men penetrate farther and farther into space. Meanwhile the romantic appeal of the remote and strange has not diminished — indeed it has been stimulated by mass media. Burton Holmes lectures still draw audiences. Movie shorts and television bring to the screen vivid pictures of life in remote lands. Magazines and Sunday supplements (not to mention the travel sections of our newspapers) print thousands of articles each year designed to interest the public in travel abroad; and periodicals like *Holiday* and *The National Geographic Magazine* flourish.

Whether or not travel literature constitutes a *genre* is a question of real, though perhaps only minor, importance. The guide book, factual, objective, impersonal, scarcely qualifies as typical; the purest examples of the travel book are reports of what a traveller has actually experienced and seen, his description of routes traversed, of the cities in which he has lodged, of the antiquities, monuments, customs, commodities, and character of the peoples among whom he has moved. It is a fascinating scholarly exercise, as Mr Philip M. Barbour has shown in his study of Captain John Smith's *True Travels* (see Appendix), to trace out routes, identify places, and fit into an authentic historical context the "tall tales" of an adventurer. True travel books are of course largely autobiographical, and are enriched with opinions and reflections of the sort which appear in Patrick Brydone's *Tour Through Sicily and Malta*. Thus, like other forms, travel literature may be, and often is, modal rather than generic — e g, the traveller's interest may be concentrated chiefly on commerce, or geography, or archaeology, or natural history, or sociology, or anthropology, or linguistics. He may be primarily concerned with the production of propaganda for colonization or conquest; he may be at heart a historian, by profession a diplomat or political observer. Professor James Osborn's illuminating essay not only reminds us how much visitors to Greece contributed to the "classical" element in English (and American) culture of the eighteenth and nineteenth centuries, but also traces the stages through which their writings helped to develop the powerful movements of Hellenism and neo-Hellenism.

It is clear that travellers may create images and establish attitudes, and the studies of Professor Herbert Barrows, who has interested himself in what nineteenth-century men of letters got from books about Italy, as well as from their own travels, are concerned with this topic. The voyager's account often suggests to the creative writer a plot for a play, or an episode for an epic; such borrowings appear, of course, in the works of Spenser, Shakespeare, and Milton. Professor William Jewkes has propounded the thesis that influences may also flow the other way, presenting evidence to show how Elizabethan voyagers incorporated motifs from heroic and romantic literature in their narratives. Most frequently, however, it is the creative writer who assimilates the traveller's themes — as Byron did in *Childe Harold*.

Many prose fictions, of course, are built upon the plan of a journey, domestic or foreign, and here again the influence of travel literature is apparent, sometimes faintly, sometimes strongly. The novel, especially the kind developed on the model of the picaresque from Defoe to Smollett (and beyond), provides many examples. In such books the fictional traveller can easily move from the observation of manners to social criticism — and may find an unfamiliar culture inferior or superior to his own. The Oriental traveller in England, as well as the English visitor to the continent of the United States, may be used to make telling points about the defects of society, and the essayist as well as the novelist has taken full advantage of the opportunities thus offered for irony and satire. The burlesque travel book likewise affords large possibilities for satiric humor — not least at the expense of the traveller. Professor Franklin Rogers has touched upon this subject, and has shown how a minor branch of literature may be connected with a much more complex and significant kind, the international novel.

No doubt the freest form which parallels true travel literature is the imaginary voyage, traditionally contrived so that it not only directs attention to the defects of human nature and human institutions but also suggests remedies. The philosophical fable, the vision of an unspoiled land peopled by noble savages, the projection of a state founded and conducted on truly rational principles — all have a respectable lineage. In our own age what is called science fiction has turned from its early preoccupation with imagined wonders and the fantastic application of newly discovered scientific principles to a concern with political and social organization, and to the problems which result from an increasing potential for the control both of men and of their environment. As the range of our discoveries extends, if it proves that we can indeed visit the corners of the moon, the lunar traveller's report will provide more than the romantic appeal of the not here and the not now; going beyond the imagined to the real, it may not be limited to the extension of current knowledge, but may enable us to explore a whole range of experiences not yet foreseen. As long as human curiosity remains unsatisfied, the traveller's tale will find an audience.

WARNER G. RICE

University of Michigan

The Literature of Travel

The Literature of Travel and the Mode
of Romance in the Renaissance

By W. T. JEWKES

The Pennsylvania State University

Who ever heard of th'Indian Peru?
Or who in venturous vessell measured
The Amazon huge river, now found trew?
Or fruitfullest Virginia who did ever vew?
— *The Faerie Queene,* Proem, BOOK II

LITTLE has ever been said about whether the prose genre labeled "The Literature of Travel" is aptly so called. The label is a convenient one, of course, but to some extent it begs an unexamined question, namely: does this genre have characteristics which we commonly associate with "literature," not in the broadest sense of all that is written, but rather in the narrower sense of the body of writing which displays the activity of the human imagination, or, to use Frye's formidable description, the body of "hypothetical verbal structures"?

Calling it a genre does not qualify it to be considered as literature, since that word really implies "category" or "type" — a convenient way of indicating that a body of writings has certain common characteristics. The question is: what are these characteristics? The subject matter of travel books is purportedly factual, but that would incline us to exclude them from the category of literature and to group them with the sciences of history and geography. Yet the best travel books have always had another characteristic which is not usually associated with the scientific description of the world and its events: an element of strong personal coloring, the stamp of subjectivity. Now if we can discern a degree of standardization in the subjective element, not in the assembly-line sense, but in the manner in which the larger literary conventions are standardized, we may hit upon a characteristic which we can justifiably call literary. Actually, a study of travel literature is appropriately like the study of cartography; as we go back in time, we find the elements of conventionalism becoming more and more prominent. In the nineteenth century, the subject-matter of travel accounts is conventionally chosen; in the eighteenth century, the manner is also conventional; and in the sixteenth and early seventeenth centuries, not only are the matter and manner conventional, but even the very aim, intention, and philosophical viewpoint of the travel writers are remarkably uniform. Compared with the travel accounts of other periods, Renaissance travel literature bears the closest resemblance to another contemporary literary genre, the romance, and to the extent that it does so, it exhibits the influence of the most basic of all literary conventions: mode.

Although we instinctively think of romance as having a very high fictional content, it is really not surprising that the travel literature of the period should be influenced by it, especially during the Elizabethan period, since the contours of what people then beheld as "real life" were unusually romantic. Ralegh, in his remarkable account of his voyage to Guiana, takes upon himself a serious defense of Mandeville's extravagances about the anthropophagi, so beloved of the Ripleys of the Middle Ages:

> Such a nation was written of by Mandeville, whose reports were holden for fables many yeeres, and since the East Indies were discovered, we find his relations true of such things as heretofore were held incredible . . . for mine owne part I saw them not, but I am resolved that so many people did not all combine, or forthinke to make such a report. (x 406) [1]

In the Proem to the second Book of *The Faerie Queene* occur Spenser's famous verses on the same subject:

> Right well I wote, most mighty Soveraine,
> That all this famous antique history
> Of some th' aboundance of an ydle braine
> Will judged be, and painted forgery,
> Rather than matter of just memory. . . .
>
> But let that man with better sence advize,
> That of the world least part to us is red;
> And daily how through hardy enterprize
> Many great regions are discovered,
> Which to late age were never mentioned . . .
>
> Yet all these were, when no man did them know,
> Yet have from wisest ages hidden beene;
> And later times thinges more unknowne shall show.
> Why then should witlesse man so much misweene,
> That nothing is but that which he hath seene?

Men like Sidney and Spenser evidently felt keenly the impact of their times as of an age in which romance formed the very stuff of life; when, in fact, there seemed to be a correspondence between the fancies of literature and the wonders of life which made it hard to distinguish between the two,

---

[1] All references cited in the text in parentheses are to the Maclehose reprint of Hakluyt's *The Principal Navigations, Voyages, Traffiques and Discoveries of the English Nation*, 1598 ed, in 12 vols (Glasgow 1903–5).

as the royal reception of Pocahontas in London will testify.[2] In fact, to any one who reads in the voluminous literature of travel, Mandeville's book

A Virginia Indian, from a painting by John White reproduced in the 1598 Hakluyt *Voyages* (Maclehose reprint 1903–05)

seems almost to pale into insignificance at times; yet although we know that the Elizabethan voyagers may have exaggerated for various reasons (for company propaganda, or to increase book sales), there is no doubt that the compilers of these accounts, Hakluyt and Purchas, had a more scholarly and less exploitational intent than Mandeville. Hakluyt himself sensed the charge of exaggeration and tried to make provision against it. "If any man object," he says, speaking of the accounts of the Friars, "that they have certaine incredible relations, I answer first that many true things may to the ignorant seem incredible." [3] This is a pretty skillful maneuver, to throw the burden of the proof on the skeptic, but the fact is that in his day at least, deeds had come to sound like fiction, and I think it no coincidence that Lodge wrote *Rosalynde* while on a voyage of discovery and pillage.

Despite the misleading label "epic" which has often been applied to the travel literature of Elizabethan England, its resemblance to romance has, of course, not escaped notice. It is often pointed out that romances most likely borrowed much superficial machinery from travel literature: the journeys, the shipwrecks, the narrow escapes, the captivities, the exotic settings,

[2] Philip Young, in a fascinating essay "The Mother of us all: Pocahontas Reconsidered," *Kenyon Review* xxiv (Summer 1962) 391–415, traces the growth of the romantic legend about Pocahontas from what appear to have been rather commonplace beginnings.

[3] In his Epistle to the Reader (i liii).

peoples, and manners. Such resemblances are fairly obvious, and where not, perspicuous scholars have pointed them out to us. But the more fundamental similarities in viewpoint and literary coloring do not seem to attract attention. If any attitude is characteristic of romance, it is the idealized picture of the self which it presents. In romance, society does not appear as a significant force at work upon the individual, as it is in comedy or tragedy. And the similarity in the way in which both the romances and many of the best travel accounts of the Elizabethan period present us with this concept of the idealized self is so striking as to warrant closer attention.

It is true that a large proportion of the material in the pages of Hakluyt and Purchas consists of ships' logs, commercial reports, and, to use Raleigh's phrase, "those long lists of unknown names, of merchant promoters, gentlemen adventurers, intending colonists, and ships' companies which give so businesslike an atmosphere to Hakluyt's pages." [4] There is, however, a large body of travel narratives, particularly those concerned not so much with trade and embassages as with accounts of discovery, colonization, and piratical warfare, the best of which show a concern for narrative effect which clearly entitles them to at least initial consideration as literature. And, more significantly, these accounts are infused with the same spirit as that which moves in the pages of the better romances: the *Arcadia, Euphues, The Faerie Queene, Menaphon,* and *Rosalynde.* In particular, the voyage accounts present us continually with figures and themes remarkably similar to those which we find in Spenser, Sidney, Lyly, and Lodge. These figures and themes represent the same idealization of experience which has such an important bearing on our conception of "the romantic," the peculiar manifestations of which are the great virtue of Elizabethan literature.

The term "heroic" is often applied to the travel literature of Elizabethan England, though usually without discrimination. The association begins with the narrators themselves. Drake is frequently singled out as a national hero. Robert Leng's report of Drake's exploits at Cadiz in 1587 calls Drake "our Ajax" and later compares him to Scipio, Hannibal, Achilles, and Hector! [5] In dedicating another account of the same adventure, Henry Haslop compares Drake to Julius Caesar at his greatest.[6] An anonymous account of the taking of Nombre de Dios in 1592 calls Sir John Burrough a man of "manifold good and heroicall parts" (VII 106). Ellis praises Frobisher in a

---

[4] *The English Voyages of the Sixteenth Century* (Glasgow 1928) 193.

[5] Reprinted in *The Camden Miscellany* v (London 1863) 1–23.

[6] *Newes out of the Coast of Spaine* (London 1587).

pompous poem in which he compares the navigator's return to that of Jason bringing home the Golden Fleece (vii 231). To become aware of how much of a romantic convention these references are we have only to recall the fate of Ralegh, and of Essex, and in reading oft-repeated complaints like those of George Best against the "greedie desire" of the promoters of the voyages which so hampered their achievment (vii 298) we realize how much these seafaring heroes were actually caught up in, and indeed actually hamstrung by, the complex situation at home. One of the most charmingly "heroic" scenes in all travel literature, the account of what happened to Drake among the Californian Indians, demonstrates very clearly the shrewd caution and uneasiness occasioned by the hero's isolation from his society, and the pressures even at that distance of its complex strictures:

> In coming towards our bulwarks and tents the sceptre-bearer began a song, observing his measures in a daunce, and that with a stately countenance. . . . When they had satisfied themselves, they made signes to our Generall to sit downe, to whom the King and divers others made several orations, or rather supplications, that he would take their province and kingdome into his hand, and become their King, making signes that they would resigne unto him the right and title of the whole land, and become his subjects. In which, to persuade us the better, the king and the rest, with one consent, and with great reverence, joyfully singing a song, did set a crowne upon his head, inriched his necke with all their chaines, and offred unto him many other thinges, honouring him by the name of Hioh, adding thereunto as it seemes, a signe of triumph: which thing our Generall thought not meete to reject, because he knew not what honour and profit it might be to our country, wherefore in the name and to the use of her Majestie, he tooke the scepter, crowne and dignitie of the said Countrey into his hands. . . . (xi 121–122)

The heroic atmosphere is there, even to the "Hioh," which is strangely echoic of the Greek "Io!," but there is a crucial reservation. Though Drake may have been compared to Achilles, it is obvious that Achilles would never have been placed in such a position.

A consideration of the general heroic atmosphere of the travel literature of Elizabethan England is not, however, very illuminating, and at times may even be misleading, since most of the allusions are to classical heroes. A far more interesting and significant observation comes to light when we consider the remarkable degree to which these travel accounts conform to the specific biases of the Renaissance concept of the hero, most familiar to us as it appears in the romances of the period. It is no coincidence that the *The Faerie Queene* was dedicated to Sir Walter Ralegh himself, that indefatigable traveler and voyage raconteur. For the ideals of conduct which are embodied in the heroic concept, and which lie at the heart of works like *The Faerie Queene* and the *Arcadia*, are in fact those which we find illuminating the pages of the best accounts of Burroughs, Grenville, Gilbert, and Cavendish. Whether the stories of their exploits in search of the Northwest passage, in pioneering colonization, in the quest of El Dorado, or in singeing the King of Spain's beard, were written by themselves or by others, the concept of the qualities of the leader, of the princely man, forms the cynosure of the narrative. "The Generall" as a title appears time and time again in accounts which are ostensibly factual narratives, and the repetitious nature of the attributes of such a figure impress upon us the well-developed, orthodox theory of conduct characteristic of the romances. Attitudes towards what is heroic change with time; that is why the term "epic" as applied to the Voyages is misleading. "No," says Kalander at the beginning of the *Arcadia* when he views the shipwrecked Musidorus, "I am no herald to enquire of men's pedigrees, it sufficeth me if I know their vertues." [7] And therein lies the essential difference betwen the Renaissance concept of honor and that of Classical or of medieval times. It marks, I suppose, the change-over from what sociologists would call a "shame culture" to a "guilt culture." The word "vertue" forms a refrain throughout the best travel narratives and the romances. Both types of literature show remarkable correspondence in the detailed characteristics of this particular concept; parallel passages prove this time and again.

The two major requisites of the virtuous man seem to have been wisdom and valor, *sapientia et fortitudo*, involving that cultivation of both the body and the mind so dear to Ascham. Describing the quality of Sir John of Bordeaux at the beginning of *Rosalynde*, Lodge writes:

> Wise he was, as holding in his head a supreme conceipt of pollicie, reaching with Nestor into the depth of all civil government; and to make his wisedome more gratious . . . his valor was no lesse than his witte, nor the stroke of his launce no less forcible.[8]

In the *Arcadia*, Daiphantus (Pyrocles) departs from the Helots to the tune of their "thinking it beyond the degree of humanitie to have a witte so far overgoing his age and such dreadful terror proceed from so excellent beautie" (p 47). The same qualities occur in N. H's description of Cavendish on his voyage of circumnavigation in 1586–1588. Cavendish, says this reporter, performed all his exploits "to the admiration of all men of Judgement"; he was

[7] Sir Philip Sidney, *The Countesse of Pembroke's Arcadia*, ed A. Feuillerat (Cambridge 1922) 15.

[8] Reprinted by Clarke Conwell (New Rochelle, N. Y. 1902) 5.

in fact a man of "invincible courage and great good government." [9] The important thing, however, was to keep these two qualities in balance; virtue is an activity, not a state. In describing the combat between Musidorus and Pyrocles in the *Arcadia*, Sidney forcefully emphasizes this point:

> Their courage was guided with skill and their skill was armed with courage; neither did their hardinesse darken their witte, nor their witte their hardinesse: both valiant as men despising death. . . . (p 42)

That passage might well have come as part of Edward Hayes' account of Sir Humphrey Gilbert on his last voyage:

> [He] did correct the intemperate humors, which before we noted to be in this Gentleman, and made unsavorie, and lesse delightfull his other manifolde vertues . . . [with the result that] he was refined, and made nearer drawing unto the image of God: so it pleased the divine will to resume him unto himselfe, whither both his and every other high and noble minde have always aspired. (vii 77)

It is this activity which is directed towards the quality of steadfastness in all things. Musidorus takes occasion to rally Pyrocles on this point in the *Arcadia*:

> A mind wel trayned and long exercized in vertue . . . doth not easily chaunge any course it once undertakes, but upon well grounded, well wayed causes . . . I have marked in you, I will not say an alteration, but a relenting truely, and a slackening of the maine career, you had so notably begon and almost performed . . . whereas you were wont in all places you came to give yourselfe vehemently to the knowledge of those thinges which might better your minde; to seek the familiaritie of excellent men in learning and souldiery; and lastly, to put all these thinges in practise both by continuall wise proceedinge, and worthie enterprises, as occasion fell for them: you now leave all those things undone: . . . and subject yourself to solitarines, the slye enimie, that doth most separate a man from well doing. (p 55)

Such an attitude is reflected almost detail for detail in George Best's eloquent description of Martin Frobisher as one "who well understood the office of a Souldier and an Englishman," and who:

> chiefly respecting the accomplishment of the cause he had undertaken (wherein the chiefe reputation and fame of a Generall and Captaine consisteth) and calling to his remembraunce the short time he had in hand, determined with this resolution to passe and recover his Port or else to burie himselfe with his attempt. (vii 342)

[9] In Hakluyt's *Voyages*, 1589 ed, 809.

The performance expected of such virtuous men was extremely versatile. Gone is the medieval chivalric concept of duties proper to classes; if anything, there is in this respect at least an approximation to the Greek ideal, where the great man is the man who is best at the things with which every one is familiar. There is a whimsical occasion for this in Lyly's *Euphues*, when Fidus describes the king of the bees:

> The Kyng himselfe not idle, goeth up and downe, entreating, threatning, commaunding, using the counsell of a sequel, but not losing the dignitie of a Prince, prefering those that labour to greater authoritie. . . .[10]

Set alongside an account of Drake's manifold activity in Walter Bigges' narrative of the voyage to the West Indies in 1589, the picture of the king of the bees forms an amusing parallel:

> I doe wrong if I should forget the good example of the Generall in this place, who to encourage others, and to hasten the getting of fresh water aboord the ships, tooke no lesse paine himselfe then the meanest . . . having alwaies so vigilant a care and foresight in the good ordering of his Fleete, accompanying them, as it is sayde, with such wonderfull travell of body, as doubtlesse had he bene the meanest person, as he was the chiefest, he had yet deserved the first place of honour. . . . (x 128)

Disciplined endurance seems to thrive best on adversity, and consequently dangerous conditions are almost a requisite for the nourishing of this kind of virtue. Sidney's concept of valor appears thus:

> As high honor is not onely gotten and borne by paine, and daunger, but must be nurst by the like, or els vanisheth as soone as it appears in the world: so naturall hunger thereof (which was in Pyrocles) suffered him not to account a resting seate of that, which ever riseth, or falleth, but still to make one action beget another; whereby his doings might send his praise to other mouthes to rebound againe true contentment to his spirite. (p 205–206)

Against this one might justifiably place the noble picture painted by Hayes in his moving account of Sir Humphrey Gilbert's last moments, and his magnificent words as the little Squirrel disappeared under the waves: "We are as neere to heaven by sea as by land" (viii 74). That is the epitome of the "witte quite devoid of ostentation" so praised in Musidorus, so prized by Castiglione.

The whole ideal of virtue finds its goal in service for the state, even unto death, if need be. In Lodge's *Rosalynde*, old Sir John of Bordeaux addressing

[10] Arber's English Reprints, No 9 (London 1934) 263.

his sons from his deathbed is an eloquent spokesman for this particular aspect of the theory of noble conduct:

> Let your countryes eare be your hearts content, and thinke that you are not borne for your selves, but to level your thoughts to be loyal to your prince, careful for your commonweale, and faythful to your friendes; so that Fraunce say, these men are as excellent in vertues, as they be exquisite in features. (p 7)

In like manner did Elizabeth speak to her sons, and her admonition rings throughout the patriotic pages of these voyages. At the end of Frobisher's voyage to the Northwest, Best tells us that she "rejoyced very, that among them there was so good order of government, so good agreement, every man so ready in his calling, to do whatsoever the Generall should command" (VII 319). We can well picture her in the role of Evarchus at the end of the *Arcadia*, and those who heard her were well aware that Elizabeth looked upon herself as the supreme Generall of these enterprises. We recall Drake receiving the Indian crown in her name; Ralegh making the Guianan Indians swear allegiance to her. Not that such service always brought ultimate reward; the sacrifice of personal aims was bound to involve the kind of disappointment which is plaintively evident in Ralegh's preface to his *Historie of the World* (1614):

> For myself, if I have in anything served my country, and prized it before my private; the general acceptation can yield me no other profit at this time than doth a fair sunshine day to a seaman after shipwrack, and the contrary no other harm than an outragious tempest after the port attained.

The gains may seem to be small when the matter is viewed in this light; yet Ralegh says elsewhere apropos the death of Sir Richard Grenville in the famous sinking of the *Revenge*:

> The comfort that remayneth to his friends is, that hee ended his life honourably in respect of the reputation wonne to his nation and countrey, and the same to his posteritie, that being dead, he hath not outlived his owne honour. (VII 48)

It is in fact these few notes of disillusionment which bring to our attention how idealized a picture we receive in such accounts. Of course, it is possible that some of the writers were flattering the great figures of the day; and when the great figures themselves wrote they may have been the consistency of attitude in these accounts of leadership and endurance; moreover their correspondence with what we find in romance can hardly be fortuitous. A moment's second thought after reading these glowing accounts soon reminds us that the actual events were not all as described. Some principle of selection is clearly at work. There are, of course, many accounts which strike a more "realistic" note. Cook's account, as well as another anonymous narrative, of Drake's voyage of circumnavigation is sharply critical of that hero; [11] Sellman quietly but firmly proves to us that Frobisher was a poor commander; [12] Linschoten tells us that Grenville's "owne people hated him and spake very hardly of him" (vii 81); Cavendish's own account of his exploits indicates that he was at best a spoiled brat, so ungracious and self-glorifying that even Purchas felt he must suppress "some passionate speeches of Master Candish against some private persons." [13] Maynarde describes Drake as "the child of fortune" and speaks in a very disabused fashion of what were Ralegh's greatest dreams:

> Like as upon the cominge of the sun, dewes and mistes begin to vanish, so our blinded eyes began now to open, and we founde that the glorious speeches, of an hundred places that they knew in the Indies to make us rich, was but a baite to draw her Majestie to give them honourable imployments and us to adventure our lives for their glory.[14]

It is a regret which every purchaser of phony oil-stock has probably voiced. Even more convincing proof of the ungallant reality is found in a private letter of Ralegh's about the Cadiz action in 1587, which was not intended for publication:

> While I was thus speaking with the Earl, the Marshall, who thought it some touch to his great esteemed valour, to ride behind me so many hours, got up ahead my ship; which my lord Thomas perceiving, headed him again, myself being but a quarter of an hour absent. At my return, finding myself from being the first to be but the third, I presently let slip anchor, and thrust in between my lord Thomas and the marshal, and went up further ahead than all them before, and thrust myself athwart the channel, so as I was sure none should outstart me again for that day. . . . The marshal, while we had no leisure to look behind us, secretly fastened a rope on my ships side towards him . . . but . . . I caused it to be cut off, and so he fell back into his place.[15]

[11] "The Voyage of Sir Francis Drake Around the World," in *The World Encompassed*, Hakluyt Society, 1st Series, No 16 (London 1854) 187–218.
[12] Reprinted by the Hakluyt Society, 1st Series, No 38 (London 1867) 290–316.
[13] In *Purchas His Pilgrimes*, 1625, reprinted by Maclehose in 20 vols (Glasgow 1905–7) xvi 148.
[14] *Sir Francis Drake His Voyage*, 1595, reprinted by the Hakluyt Society, 1st Series, No 4 (London 1849) 1–22.
[15] See *The Complete Works of Sir Walter Ralegh, Kt.* (Oxford 1829) viii 671–672.

An unguarded confidential moment emphasizes very forcefully the romantic coloring which was consistently applied to the material of life in the concept of the heroic figure who dominates these travel accounts.

If life aboard ship made one aware of the paradoxical aspects of a tightly organized social structure, life in the wild uninhabited areas to which the voyagers came brought to mind the paradox of nature, and revived again the concept of the noble savage with its attendant dreams of the Golden Age and the Fortunate Isles. Such a theme is also essentially a romantic one, and survives in Renaissance romance as the pastoral element. William Empson believes that the pastoral, which implies "a beautiful relation between rich and poor," is a natural accompaniment of an heroic theme.[16] For the hero, if he includes everybody, is tempted to see part of himself, that which precedes his education, as the primitive man. The idea of nature in the ancients posits a kind of ethical norm which is antecedent to all political law and which is another form of projection of the idealized self. Such an idea is voiced by Euphues in reply to the old man who counsels him:

> Nature was had in such estimation and admiration among the Heathen people, that she was reputed for the onely Godesse in heaven: If Nature then have largely and bountifully endewed me with hir gyftes, why deeme you me so untoward and graceless? If she have dealt hardely with me, why extoll you so much my byrth? If nature beare no sway, why use you this adulation? If nature worke the effect, what booteth any education? (p 42)

The latter part of that speech, though used sophistically by Euphues on that occasion, nevertheless displays the paradoxical nature of conclusions drawn by a highly civilized man when he looks both at the evils of civilization and the pleasant aspects of primitive life. The paradox is most fully developed in Spenser, where on the one hand the "salvage nation" almost slays Serena, while on the other hand she is succored by the "gentle salvage." But the attitude is implicit also in the *Arcadia*. Philanax in the same speech can voice his lack of prejudice against country people, and his disapproval of Basilius committing Pamela to the care of Dametas (p 28–29).

There are in fact two attitudes at work — sometimes separately, sometimes in paradoxical juxtaposition — in the views of nature and the natural man, expressed in both Elizabethan travel literature and romance. The idea of the naturally good man, which is a vestige of the chronological primitivism

---

[16] *Some Versions of Pastoral* (London 1935) 11.

of the legends of the Golden Age, can be found frequently in the accounts
of the voyages. Barlowe in his narrative of his voyage to Virginia with
Amidas in 1584 introduces us to an idyllic people:

> We found the people most gentle, loving and faithfull, voide of all guile
> and treason, and such as live after the manner of the golden age. (vII 305)

How much of an idealization this was can be guessed from the fact that the
guileful Barlowe, when the natives showed him pearls, feigned indifference
until he learned their source. Barlowe then goes on to describe a veritable
Garden of Eden with an abundance of fish and timber, and a fertile soil:

> We found such plentie as well there as in all places else, both on the
> sand and on the greene soile on the hils, as in the plaines, as well on
> every little shrubbe, as also climing towardes the tops of high cedars,
> that I thinke in all the world the like abundance is not to be found.
> (vIII 298)

Brereton's account of Gosnold's voyage to Virginia in 1602, a voyage which
ended on Cape Cod, is equally idyllic in describing the natives:

> These people, as they are exceeding courteous, gentle of disposition, and
> well-conditioned, excelling all others that we have seene; so for shape of
> bodie and lovely favour, I thinke they excell al the people of America.
> They are quick eied, and stedfast in the looks, fearelesse of others harmes,
> as intending none themselves . . . .[17]

This also is a highly romanticized account, since another narrative of the
same voyage tells us that these very colonists had to return home only three
months later because of heavy losses from attacks by the fierce and treacher-
ous natives.[18]

Often such native peoples are depicted as hardly in need of civilization,
though not without an awe for some of its aspects. In describing the Eskimos
which Davis met on his search for the Northwest Passage in 1585, Jane
states:

> They tooke great care one of another; for when we had bought their
> boats, then two other would come and carry him betweene them that
> had sold us his. They are a very tractable people, voide of craft or double-
> dealing, and easie to be brought to any civility or good order; but we
> judge them to be idolaters and to worship the Sunne. (vII 388)

---

[17] Reprinted in *Sailors' Narratives of Voyages Along the New England Coast,* ed G. P. Winship
(Boston 1935) 45.
[18] *Purchas His Pilgrimes* xvIII 302–313.

The last phrase sounds dutiful but unconvinced. That remarkable passage about Drake's reception by the Californian Indians which I quoted earlier itself reads like an echo of Spenser's description of how the salvages treated Una:

> Their harts she ghessed by their humble guise,
> And yeelds her to extremetie of time:
> So from the ground she fearlesse doth arise,
> And walketh forth without suspect of crime.
> They all as glad as birdes of joyous Pryme,
> Thence lead her forth, about her dauncing round,
> Shouting, and singing all a shepheard's ryme;
> And with green braunches strowing all the ground,
> Do worship her as Queene with olive girlond cround. (I vi 13)

Both the romances and the travel literature are inclined to take this particular way of regarding the noble savage idea to the very verge of absurdity, where the savage actually excels the civilized man in so many ways as to cast complete doubt on the values of civilization. In Book VI of *The Faerie Queene*, the salvages are about to make a bloody sacrifice of Serena, but refuse to violate her because, says Spenser, "religion held even theeves in measure" (VI viii 43).

But an even more curiously ambiguous picture occurs in Ralegh's description of the King of the Emira Indians, whom he encountered in his voyage to Guiana in 1595:

> The King of this land is called Carpana, a man very wise, subtill, and of great experience, being little lesse than an hundred yeeres olde: in his youth he was sent by his father into the Island of Trinidad . . . at that place in his youth hee had seen many Christians . . . by reason whereof he grew of more understanding, and noted the difference of nations, comparing the strength and armes of his countrey with those of the Christians, and ever after temporized so, as whosoever els did amisse, or was wasted by contention, Carpana kept himself and his countrey in quiet and plenty. . . . (x 372)

It appears that the old native learned early from the Christians' bad example what not to do. The same strain runs to an even more striking degree in his description of the great King Topiawari:

> This Topiawari is helde for the prowdest, and wisest of all the Orenoquepoui, and so hee behaved himselfe towardes mee in all his answeres at my returne, and I marveilled to finde a man of that gravitie and judgment, and of so good discourse, that had no helpe of learning nor breede. (x 401)

As White comments on the larger passage from which this is extracted:

> There is a suggestion of Sir Thomas More's *Utopia* in Ralegh's reference
> to a discussion with Topiawari, the old Indian king, who apparently pro-
> vided the same kind of information about the strange and wonderful
> land of Guiana that Raphael Hythloday gave about Utopia when he
> was talking to More and Peter Giles.[19]

The paradox raised by this exaggerated treatment can be solved in one of
two ways. Spenser solves it one way, in an aristocratic manner, by discovering that his gentle salvage is in fact born of noble blood. But the problem
can also be solved by pointing out that such a view of man is only chrono-
logically primitive, not culturally, and by equating such simplicity with the
life of reason, rather than with the absence of civilization. Actually, by
presenting us with both noble and vicious savages, Spenser is able to make
a valuable point. As one critic puts it:

> He pictures savages at their best realizing completely their animal-like
> potentialities, in order to show that men should fully realize their rational
> potentialities. He then pictures savages at their most brutish, to show
> to just what bestial depths men who forget that they are men can sink.[20]

The latter solution may seem more satisfactory, because less artificial, but
both solutions are essentially romantic, since they place great stress on the
ideal capacities of the developed self. The result of what Spenser is aiming
at can be observed in Ralegh's treatment of the Indians in Guiana:

> But I protest before the majestie of the living God, that I neither know
> nor beleeve, that any of our company one or other, by violence or other
> wise, ever knew any of their women, and yet we saw many hundreds,
> and had many in our power, and of those very yong, and excellently well
> favoured, which came among us without deceit, starke naked.
>
> Nothing got us more love amongst them then this usage: for I suffered
> not any of them to take from any of the nations so much as a Pina, or a
> Potato roote, without giving them contentment. . . . But I confess it was
> a very impatient worke to keepe the meaner sort from spoyle and stealing,
> when we came to their houses: which because in all I could not prevent,
> I caused my Indian interpreter at every place we departed to knowe of
> the losse or wrong done, and if ought were stolen or taken by violence,
> either the same was restored, and the partie punished in their sight, or
> else was payed for to their uttermost demand. . . . (x 391)

---

[19] W. B. White, "The Narrative Technique of the Elizabethan Voyage and Travel Literature,"
unpublished dissertation (Lehigh University 1955) 159.

[20] R. H. Pearce, "Primitivistic Ideas in *The Faerie Queene*," *JEGP* xliv (1945) 142.

Ralegh may be protesting too much, but clearly he is expressing the view that civilized man may employ his art and skill in refining upon and developing nature. He cannot surpass nature, but perhaps he can better fulfill her potentialities.

Examples of such a complex view are rare in Elizabethan travel literature, but by no means unique. They indicate an idealistic view in sharp contrast to the realistic accounts which abound with superstitious and vicious attitudes to native treachery and cruelty, or which, like Edward Hayes' preface to his narrative of Gilbert's last voyage, ponderously preach the value of Christianity in making the natives better men.

Lest the examination of parallel texts become tedious, I shall take it that they have fully demonstrated how factual matter may be treated in a manner and from a viewpoint which we can only define as literary in the narrow sense, and that it is the clear influence of the romantic mode of viewing experience which best entitles these travel accounts to the label of "literature." One item of interest remains: the discovery of a theoretical explanation for the way in which these voyage raconteurs approached and used their material. The answer can in part be found in the literary criticism of the period, particularly in Sidney. In the celebrated *Apology*, Sidney lays remarkable stress on the transforming power of the poetic imagination:

> Only the Poet, disdeining to be tied to any such subjection, lifted up with the vigor of his own inuention, doth grow in effect into another nature: in making things either better than nature bringeth foorth, or quite a new, formes such as never were in nature, as the *Heroes, Demigods, Cyclops, Chymeras, Furies*, and such like; so as he goeth hand in hand with nature, not enclosed within the narrow warrant of her gifts, but freely raunging within the Zodiack of his owne wit.[21]

In consequence, argues Sidney, nature has never brought forth "a truer lover than Theagenes." The astonishing innovation in English critical thought in the first part of the passage I quoted above is reiterated a page later, when he asserts that the poet "bringeth things foorth surpassing her [i.e., nature's] doings." Shortly thereafter, this idea is restated in an even more extravagant form, subject to only a single qualification, when he claims that in imitating, poets "borrow nothing of what is, hath bin, or shall be, but range onely reined with learned discretion into the divine consideration of what may be, and should be." [22]

[21] Sigs B4v, C1r (Facsimile Text Society Reprint, New York 1928).
[22] Sig C2v. This view had, of course, already found voice on the Continent in the writings of Daniello, Scaliger, and Minturno, though my impression is that none of these took as extreme a position as Sidney.

The significance of Sidney's viewpoint in the *Apology for Poetry* has not, I think, been sufficiently noted.[23] What he is doing, in fact, is laying the foundation for a romantic theory of literature; he treats imagination and insight as though they are indistinguishable, as in C. M. Bowra's description of their relationship for the Romantic poets, "for all practical purposes a single faculty." [24] Bowra sees contradictions in the attitude of Renaissance artists concerning this matter, contradictions epitomized in Shakespeare's conflicting epithets for the poetic imagination: "airy nothing" and "something of great constancy." Contradictions there may be, not only in Shakespeare, but even in Sidney (compare with the passages I have been quoting his strange objections to the Elizabethan drama) but it is erroneous to claim, as Bowra does, that:

> Though Elizabethans excelled almost all other ages in the creation of imaginary worlds, their greatest thinkers made no great claim for them and were on the whole content that they should do no more than give a respite from the cares of ordinary life. (p 6)

The point about these contradictions is that the new expressive viewpoint had not yet won over the older pragmatic one. Consequently, for Sidney, the imaginative faculty is not an end in itself, as it became in the more extreme theories of the later Romantic poets, but rather a means to an end. The end of literature is definitely to be found in the world of action:

> What so much good doth teaching bring foorth . . . as that it mooveth one to do that which it doth teach. For as Aristotle saith, it is not γνωσις but πραξις must be the frute; and how πραξις can be without being moved to practice is no hard matter to consider. (E1$^{r, v}$)

The test, ultimately, of whether the poet's fancy is building "castles in the aire" or has moral substance, is in the effect achieved:

> So farre substancially it worketh, not onely to make a *Cyrus*, which had been but a particular excellency as nature might have done, but to bestow a *Cyrus* upon the world to make many *Cyrusses*, if they will learne aright, why and how that maker made him. (C1^r)

The romantic attitude towards experience can, then, by working through literature, actually shape the matter of life into a pattern like that of romance.

---

[23] I note only one comment on it. David Daiches observes that "for Sidney, the ideal world of the poet is of value because it is both a better world than the real one and it is presented in such a way that the reader is stimulated to try and imitate it in his own practice." *Critical Approaches to Literature* (Englewood Cliffs, NJ 1957) 59.

[24] *The Romantic Imagination* (Cambridge, Mass 1957) 7.

An extravagant claim, we may think, but we have the testimony of Sidney's celebrated death at Zutphen in its support.

This peculiar blend of the expressive and the pragmatic valuations of literature does not find open expression elsewhere in English criticism. The writers themselves mostly admit to only pragmatic justification. "The generall end, therefore, of all the booke," writes Spenser of *The Faerie Queene*, "is to fashion a gentleman or noble person in vertuous and gentle discipline." Lodge's *Rosalynde* closes with a clear explication of what aristocratic morals

The Black Pinnace in which Sir Philip Sidney's body was carried for his funeral. Drawing by Thomas Lant, London 1587; engraving in the 1598 Hakluyt *Voyages* (here reproduced from the Maclehose reprint)

the gentlemen readers may see in the story he has just told. And although the pastoral implications of Sidney's title have somewhat obscured a clear impression of the *Arcadia*, it is definitely a heroic romance, with very little pastoral in it, and a fit example of Sidney's own precepts.[25] And a similar purpose is avowed by many travel narrators. Hakluyt's preface I have already mentioned, and I will only include two more examples. Sir Francis Drake, nephew of the great circumnavigator, tells us on the title-page of his account of his uncle's exploits that he wrote it "for the stirring up of heroicall spirits." And Henry Roberts designs his account of Sir James Lancaster's voyage to Brazil "that our brave-minded youthes, in tyme to come, seeing what hath ben done by men of our time, may imitate the vertues, and endevoring to deserve, like him, honor in his cuntry, and remaine a terror to all his

[25] See Marcus S. Goldman, *Sir Philip Sidney and the "Arcadia,"* Univ of Illinois Studies in Language and Literature XVII (1934) 156–157.

enimies." [26] Such work would be worthy of Xenophon, whose history Sidney praised, because of its imaginative content, as an "absolute heroicall Poeme" (C3ʳ). Sir Walter Raleigh appropriately sums up this attitude in Elizabethan life and letters: "In those days, the poets and the men of action vied with each other in the effort to outshine deeds with words, and to impoverish words with deeds." [27]

Actually, the spirit which animates all these works is not the dry didacticism which the writers suggest. Though less explicit about it, it is apparent that for them, as for Sidney, the pragmatic end justifies any means, and the means they employ is in fact the romantic poetic imagination of which he is the first eloquent exponent. We are left then with the clear impression that because of their often openly avowed idealistic intentions, and because of the romantic mode of viewing life which fills their pages with aristocratic heroes and noble savages, the best travel accounts of the English Renaissance were regarded by both their writers and readers as, in those respects, indeed worthy of the title "literature." For in the Elizabethan view, literature fills an important function in keeping the two aspects of life, active and contemplative, in balance. It fulfills, in the romantic interpretation, a kind of double purpose. By expressing the noblest imaginative aspirations of man, it can aid him in the contemplation of his divine possibilities and prospects; but the particular way in which it works, by presenting pictures of heroic figures in action, can inspire man to further action, to leave his books and seek to model his life on them, to make it a living imitation of romance.

---

[26] Reprinted by the Hakluyt Society, 2nd Series, No 85 (London 1940) 57.
[27] *The English Voyages of the Sixteenth Century* (Glasgow 1928) 188.

Travel Literature and the Rise of
Neo-Hellenism in England

By James M. Osborn
Yale University

APPROPRIATELY, this paper begins with a quotation from Sir George Wheler. For two centuries the mainland of Greece had been virtually sealed off from the states of Europe when in 1675 Wheler, a young Oxford graduate on the Grand Tour, accompanied by a French travelling companion, ventured to land in Attica where he filled notebooks with accounts of the antiquities and the present state of the Greek people. To their surprise, though some voyagers had asserted that little besides the Acropolis remained, they found Athens to be a populous and comparatively well organized city. Wheler complained that these travellers "perhaps have seen it [Athens] only from the Sea, through the wrong end of their Perspective-Glass." The thesis offered in this paper is similar — that writers on Neo-Hellenism in England also have tended to look "through the wrong end of the Perspective-Glass." [1]

Despite the extensive list of writings on Neo-Hellenism in France and Germany,[2] no book on Neo-Hellenism in England appeared until 1931, when Harvard University published the Bowdoin Prize Essay for that year, written by an undergraduate named Harry Levin. Titled *The Broken Column, A Study in Romantic Hellenism*, the essay is an inquiry into the changes that affected the classical tradition in the romantic age. By examining the concept of Greece held by various Germans from Winckelmann to Herder, and French writers from the Abbé Barthélemy to Renan, and in

---

[1] Sir George Wheler, *A Journey into Greece* (1682) 347.

[2] Neo-Hellenism may be defined as the revival of interest in ancient Greek civilization, based on the conviction that it made a peculiar and lasting contribution to Western culture. Among studies on French aspects, the following may be mentioned: Louis Bertrand, *La fin du classicisme et le retour à l'antique dans la seconde moitié du XVIIIe siècle et les premières années du XIXe, en France* (Paris 1897); Demetrius Bikélas, "Le Philhellénisme en France," *Revue d'Histoire Diplomatique* v 346–365 (Paris 1891); René Bray, *La formation de la doctrine classique en France* (Paris 1927); Nicholas Torga, *Les voyageurs Français dans l'Orient Européen* (Paris 1928); Le Comte de Laborde, *Athènes aux XVe, XVIe, et XVIIe siècles*, 2 vols (Paris 1854); Jean Longnon, "Quatre siècles de philhellénisme français," *La Revue de France* i (No 6) 512–542; Émile Malakis, *French Travellers in Greece, 1770–1820: An Early Phase of French Philhellenism* (Philadelphia 1925). For Neo-Hellenism in Germany see: Karl Borinski, *Die Antike in Poetik und Kunsttheorie von Ausgang des klassischen Altertums bis auf Goethe und Wilhelm von Humboldt* (Leipzig 1914–24); E. M. Butler, *The Tyranny of Greece over Germany* (London 1935); Humphrey Trevelyan, *The Popular Background of Goethe's Hellenism* (London 1934); Hans Meyer, et al, *Kulturwissenschaftliche Bibliographie zum Nachleben der Antike* (Leipzig and Berlin 1931–34).

more detail the attitudes of Byron, Keats and Shelley, the young author provided a comprehensive panorama of the subject. The essay made a welcome contribution to the study of romanticism, within the limitations of its size and scope.

Levin's influence is acknowledged in the opening sentence of Bernard H. Stern's *The Rise of Romantic Hellenism in English Literature 1732–1786* (1940). Although only fifty years are staked out for examination, Stern's study ranges beyond the announced dates, and also beyond English literature to archeology and the aesthetics of Winckelmann. He also has a chapter on "Romantic Hellenism and the Literature of Travel to the East," most of which consists of quotations.

The next important book appeared in 1943, Stephen A. Larrabee's *English Bards and Grecian Marbles*. The rest of the title indicates the special area covered: "The Relationship Between Sculpture and Poetry, Especially in the Romantic Period." Although thus limited to one aspect of the larger subject, Larrabee provides many perceptive remarks on the history of taste.

The fourth book (and the first outside America) is Terence Spencer's *Fair Greece, Sad Relic*, published in 1954. The subtitle describes its scope as "Literary Philhellenism from Shakespeare to Byron," which the Introduction explains as "a survey of the literary contacts between England and the modern country of Greece during the three centuries preceding the romantic enthusiasm which greeted the Greek national revival in the early nineteenth century." The author has thrown his net far and wide (no reference to a Turk in early drama escapes him) but has synthesized well the broad aspects of his subject. Spencer stands on the shoulders of his American predecessors, and *Fair Greece, Sad Relic* may be considered the definitive book on Philhellenism.

To return to "the wrong end of the Perspective-Glass" my contention is that Levin, Stern, Larrabee and Spencer have looked at Neo-Hellenism through the reverse end of the historical telescope. Their books are concerned with romanticism first and with Neo-Hellenism primarly as an aspect of romanticism. Moreover, being literary critics, these four authors discuss Neo-Hellenism chiefly as a literary event. Their attitude can even be called belletristic, for they focus on the best poets, though poetry represents only one of the manifestations of Neo-Hellenism.

My reading of the subject has led to several conclusions: first that Neo-Hellenism passed through three recognizable phases. The "bookish" Hellenism of neo-classicism, which characterized the seventeenth century gave way to the first phase of Neo-Hellenism, which may be called Archaeography, the systematic description of antiquities. (Archaeology, the term used by some writers, is unsatisfactory because of its implication of excavations, particularly in prehistorical sites). The Archaeographical phase lasted well into the second half of the eighteenth century, when the romantic element, present from the beginning, became dominant. This second phase is Romantic Hellenism, so named by Levin and his followers. The third phase occurred when Philhellenism became the foremost element: romantic

The Acropolis, drawn by "Athenian" Stuart about 1753.
James Stuart and Nicholas Revett, *Antiquities of Athens* (London 1762–1830) vol II ch 1 plate 1 detail

sentiments towards the ancient Greeks were superseded by political sentiments towards the modern Greeks, sympathy for them in their struggle for independence from the Turks. In all three phases, each of the three elements is found; though each in turn becomes dominant.

My second contention is that Neo-Hellenism should be viewed in a chronological perspective, beginning with the renewal of contact with Greece by travellers in the seventeenth century and continuing with their followers in succeeding generations.

Thirdly, I believe that Neo-Hellenism is best understood by focusing on the means by which these travellers communicated with the general public, namely through the books they wrote about Greece, for travel literature was then, as it is now, a popular literary genre.

The first phase in "the rise of Neo-Hellenism in England" begins with the hero of our opening paragraph, Sir George Wheler. Before he set foot on the Greek mainland ("dry Greece" as it is called, in contrast to "wet Greece," the myriad Greek islands) English travellers had been rare indeed. Although ships visited Zante, Crete, Rhodes, Cyprus, Chios and other islands, as well as Smyrna and other Asia Minor ports, few of them risked calls on the mainland of Greece, especially the peninsular areas south of the Dus massif, where most of the history celebrated as the "glory that was Greece" took place. Professor Warner G. Rice, in his pioneering study of "Early English Travellers to Greece and the Levant," [3] written earlier than Levin's *Broken Column* though published two years later, reports only six Englishmen who visited Athens or the peninsular mainland, some of them on second-hand evidence.[4] To these I can add only three others who were there before 1675.[5] That year marks a milestone, for in June of that year Wheler, the young Oxford graduate, having sometime earlier parted company with George Hickes, his learned tutor while at Lincoln College, teamed up with a new travelling companion, Jacob Spon, a Doctor of the Faculty of Paris, who had practised medicine in Lyons, but had spent half a year in Rome studying antiquities. In fact, before leaving Lyons in 1674 Spon had published the first account of Athens by any eyewitness among the early travellers. This was in the form of a long letter from the French Jesuit, Jacques Paul Babin, dated 8 October from Smyrna, addressed to the Abbé Pecoil of Lyons. Spon supplied some notes and a preface and published the letter as *Relation de l'État Présent de la Ville d'Athènes*. It fired the French physician with a desire to visit Greece, an ardor which he communicated to Wheler. The young Englishman had inherited a modest income, sufficient to allow

[3] University of Michigan *Essays and Studies in English and Comparative Literature* (Ann Arbor 1933).

[4] John Erigena in the ninth century, on the testimony of William of Malmesbury (p 206); Anthony Jenkinson and John Sanderson in Elizabethan times (p 213); the painful perigrine, William Lithgow who was in Greece about 1610; William Petty, sent by Sir Thomas Roe to look for marbles in Athens; and another agent (or Petty?) dispatched by Sir Thomas to the Peloponnese (p 252, 255).

[5] Master John of Basingstoke, Archdeacon of Leicester in the early thirteenth century, is said by Matthew Paris to have studied in Athens. Lord Winchelsea, Ambassador to the Sublime Porte, stopped there late in 1668 and a few months later sent a frieze to England. The traveller Bernard Randolph, who cruised about the Levant on several voyages, visited the mainland in 1674, though his *Present State of the Morea* did not reach print until 1686. Quite possibly three other Englishmen also visited Athens: Sir Paul Rycaut, while secretary to Lord Winchelsea, Lord Henry Howard (later sixth Duke of Norfolk) on his return from a visit to Constantinople in 1664, and the traveller Edward Brown.

him to concur in the venture to Greece and Constantinople, and to pay the expenses of the "discreet and ingenious" Dr Spon.[6]

Two circumstances serve as concomitants to make 1675 a felicitous time for Wheler and Spon to have embarked on their journey. The first concerns the French Ambassador to the Porte, the Marquis de Nointel, who had visited Athens in the previous year. Thus when Wheler and Spon reached Constantinople in the autumn of 1675, the French Ambassador was able to describe to them in detail the present state of Athens and the Acropolis. Their eyes must have blazed when he showed them the drawings of the frieze on the Parthenon, executed at the Ambassador's direction by an artist named Jacques Carrey.[7] Here was first hand evidence of what the young travellers could expect to find, and practical advice about how to venture into this Turkish stronghold: evidence and advice of equal value they could not have found elsewhere, or at any earlier time.

The second concomitant circumstance was the acquisition of a book recently arrived from Paris,[8] which Wheler and Spon pored over while awaiting departure in Venice, and studied repeatedly as they voyaged among the Greek islands and the cities of Asia Minor before they finally landed on the mainland of Greece about New Year's day, 1676. Published under the name of Monsieur de la Guilletière and with the title *Athènes ancienne et nouvelle* (1675) the book gave a remarkable account of the city, its people and its antiquities. The young travellers hung on every point, of which only a few can be quoted here.[9]

The narrative whisks the reader about from one detail to another that twentieth-century travellers may recognize: one street, he tells us, is occupied mainly by shoemakers; the list of chief families reads like a directory of streets in modern Athens; the bright Greek schoolboys excel at their lessons; the conversational vivacity of the citizens prompted the remark, "We attributed much of their vigour to their diet, and their use of Honey, which

[6] Besides their enthusiasm for antiquities the friends had at least two other bonds of interest. The first, surprisingly, was religion, for Dr Spon held strong Protestant views and Wheler had decided before embarking on his travels to enter Holy Orders on his return. He ultimately became a Prebendary of Durham Cathedral and the author, among other worthy works, of *The Protestant Monastery; or Christian Oeconomicks, containing Directions for the Religious Conduct of a Family* (1698). The second, perhaps equally surprising, was science, for Wheler had been from childhood an ardent and observant botanist.

[7] Wheler, *Journey*, p 362. Carrey's drawings were first reproduced in the Abbé Barthélémy's *Les Voyages du jeune Anacharsis* in 1791, in miniature. The first enlarged reproductions were in Vol IV of the *Antiquities of Athens*, 1816.

[8] It was licensed 13 Dec 1674 and registered 4 Jan 1675.

[9] From the English translation that appeared promptly in 1676 under the title, *An Account of a Late Voyage to Athens, Containing the Estate both Ancient and Modern of that Famous City . . . now Englished.*

the Athenians use very frequently, being excellently good. Their physicians account their Honey the wholsomest of their food . . . " (p 147).

Thus Wheler and Spon were well prepared when in January 1676 they approached Athens. Fortunately, they were able to stay with Jean Giraud, a Frenchman who served as the British consul. Wheler and Spon remained a month, each day crammed with observing details about Greek people, Greek antiquities and local botany.[10] But it did not take these two keen-eyed travellers long — especially Dr Spon — to ascertain that Monsieur de la Guilletière was a literary fiction, and the book a fake. The author, one Guillet,[11] possessed a gift of style, thanks to which the book has a vivacity, a narrative flow, and sense of veracity that remind one of Defoe. Sooner or later someone would have exposed the fraud, though if Wheler and Spon had not arrived so promptly on the classic ground with their measuring rods, while their host, the worthy consul Giraud, was still alive, the exposure of the fabrication might have been more difficult.

After returning to their respective homelands both young men published accounts of their travels. Dr Spon, who wrote with an easy flow of mind, produced in 1678 three volumes under the title, *Voyage d'Italie, de Dalmatie, de Grèce et du Levant . . . par Iacob Spon, Docteur Médecin Aggregé à Lyon, & avec George Wheler Gentilhomme Anglois.* Wheler, more phlegmatic as well as more naive than his Gallic companion, did not bestir himself until the success of Spon's book brought the threat of an English translation. Wheler's response, with a reciprocal bow to his French colleague, appeared as a folio volume published in November 1682 with the title *A Journey into Greece . . . In Company of Dr Spon of Lyons.* In his preface Wheler states that he found Spon's text so consistent with his own notebooks that he had been content to translate it with few changes, principally the addition of many botanical observations. The book was dedicated to Charles II, who responded by conferring a knighthood on the author.

Its publication was indeed a noteworthy event, for Spon and Wheler were the first travellers since Pausanias in the second century A D to give a careful description of Greek antiquities. Later generations are particularly

---

[10] In his preface Wheler observed, *"I know some will say, why does he treat us with insiped descriptions of Weeds, and make us hobble after him over broken stones, decayed buildings, and old rubbish?"*

[11] He had developed a correspondence with the Capuchin missionaries in Athens, and based his account on information received from them, printing for the first time a map of Athens that had been sent to the Capuchin headquarters in Paris. Guillet also had corresponded with Giraud, who had been consul to the French before he shifted his services to the British. He then embellished the current information with details gleaned from the ancients. (Fortunately these had been collected by Johannes Meiersuis, professor of Greek at Leyden, in his *Athenae Atticae,* 1624.)

indebted to their description of the Parthenon before bombardment by the Venetians reduced it to ruins in 1686. The books were deservedly popular and remained authoritative for over a century. Spon's volumes were reprinted six times, including editions in Dutch, German, and Italian. Despite the availability of the French editions of Spon, Wheler's book was translated into French in 1689 and republished in 1734.

The significance of this travel book (for it is essentially one book, published in two versions) as an event in the origins of Neo-Hellenism in Europe cannot be overestimated. Of the two travellers, the precedence undoubtedly belongs to Dr Spon. Indeed, as noted earlier, Spon's edition of Brother Babin's report on Athens in 1674, before he met Wheler in Rome, with his preface and notes, may be cited as the overture to the whole Neo-Hellenic revival. Spon's published account of his travels influenced at first or second hand every serious student of Greek antiquities for four generations, and it is still a source book that cannot be neglected. Further, his exposure of the faked narrative of Guillet resulted in fanning interest in Athens. Thus Spon's and Wheler's report offered the fresh interest of travellers into unexplored territories, into what had been a virtually blank space on the map.[12]

In the first half of the eighteenth century many Englishmen visited the Levant, for the rise of British sea power during the war of the Spanish Succession opened up the Mediterranean to trade, especially for the sale of English cloth. The Embassy at Constantinople was considered the highest diplomatic post under the British Crown, both in importance and emoluments. The English factory at Smyrna, the chief center of the Levant Company, even in Wheler's day, consisted of about a hundred persons, many of them sons of gentlemen apprenticed to merchants. In their goings and comings they visited many of the islands, and from Smyrna they made excursions to Ephesus and other nearby ruins in Asia Minor,[13] but very few of them visited "dry Greece." Perhaps the most surprising example is Aaron Hill, the future projector and pompous dramatist, who at the age of fifteen voyaged to Constantinople to visit his relative, Lord Paget, the British Ambassador to the Porte. Hill returned with Lord Paget three years later (1703)

---

12 Guillet, who had already profited from three editions of his book in 1675, did not retreat before Spon's exposé, but counterattacked in a booklet that questioned whether Spon himself had ever been in Greece. In the exchanges that followed Guillet managed to obscure the issue so successfully that his fraudulent travel book was cited seriously by a learned British Hellenist as late as 1810 (Edward Clarke, in his *Travels* III ii sec 2, 472).

13 For example, Edmund Chishull, British Chaplain at Smyrna, 1698–1702, whose *Travels in Turkey and back to England* were not published until 1747.

and in 1709 published *A Full Account of the Present State of the Ottoman Empire,* a volume of florid writing that went into a second edition, but is worthless as a source of information. Similarly, Lady Mary Wortley Montagu, on the return journey in 1718 after her husband's term as Ambassador, had their fifty-gun frigate anchor off the Troad. Afterwards she sailed among the Isles of Greece, but did not stop on the mainland, then newly reconquered by the Turks from the Venetians. Lady Mary's emotive response to reading Homer on the Trojan plains was not available to readers, however, until after her death five decades later.[14]

Two young aristocrats followed Wheler's example and extended the Grand Tour to include Greece. In 1738 another Montagu, John, fourth Earl of Sandwich (1718–1792) embarked with a company of friends on a voyage that brought them to Athens. The twenty-year-old Earl had the foresight to bring along the French artist, Jean Étienne Liotard, "to preserve in their memories, by the help of painting, these noble remains of antiquity they went in quest of." Here again, the printed account of *A Voyage Performed by the late Earl of Sandwich round the Mediterranean in the Years 1738 and 1739. Written by himself,* did not reach the public until 1799, seven years after the Earl's death. A similar expedition was made in 1749 by another future statesman, James Caulfield (1728–1799) fourth Viscount and later first Earl of Charlemont. Like Sandwich, Charlemont was accompanied by young friends, a classical tutor and an artist named Richard Dalton. The latter's folio volume of *Views in Greece, Egypt and Italy,* published in 1752, provided Englishmen with their first engravings of the Parthenon sculptures. Charlemont himself published nothing on Greece until 1790, when after years in the center of Irish politics, he gave one paper at the Royal Irish Academy.

The only important published travel book during this period was *A View of the Levant: particularly of Constantinople, Syria, Egypt and Greece,* 1743, reporting the first-hand observations of Charles Perry M D (1698–1780) in the years 1739–1742. His full description of the ruins of Greece was the first since those of Spon and Wheler to be written by an actual observer.

Less significant than Perry's book are the two volumes of Richard Pococke's *Description of the East* (1743, 1745). He had visited Athens for ten days in 1740, and the nine-page description in his second volume brings to mind Gibbon's remark that Pococke "too often confounded what he had seen with what he had heard." The plates are particularly inept: he shows

---

[14] Her *Letters* were first published in 1763, the year after her death.

the Thesium with tall thin pillars, and the westernmost caryatid of the Erechtheum facing west, with her back turned to her sisters.

The year 1744 saw the publication of *The Travels of the late Charles Thompson Esq; Containing his Observations on . . . Turkey in Europe . . . and Many parts of the World,* a work so popular that four more editions were called for within the next few decades. But like his predecessor, Monsieur de la Guilletière, Thompson is a fictional character. The book reminds us that we are discussing the age of *Robinson Crusoe* and George Psalmanzar; it is a cento of paraphrased passages from other authors, especially the French. For it should not be forgotten that the English were eager readers of French travel books, both in the original language and in translation, though none of them aside from Dr Spon's is significant enough to examine here.

The most important event of the Archaeographic phase had its beginnings in 1748. Rome was then the mecca for students of the arts who flocked there from all parts of Europe, especially from England. The neo-classical style of the French Academy was dying, and the young men either looked more deeply into the classic ideal, or turned away from it entirely. The shift from neo-classicism to the antique was stimulated by the spade, for Cardinal Albani and a number of other arbiters of taste learned how to turn marble into gold. The new excavations at Herculaneum in 1738 fanned a flame of interest in the antique that was augmented by the treasures uncovered at Pompeii a decade later. Sometime earlier, connoisseurs had adopted the attitude that Greek artists were superior to their Roman followers, and the architecture and art objects found at Herculaneum and Pompeii deflated the grandeur of Augustan Rome that the Renaissance had dreamed of. The time had come to look back to the origins of classicism, to Greece from whence Roman art and architecture were now recognized to have derived.

This was the situation in 1748 when two young British artists in Rome, James Stuart and Nicholas Revett, issued proposals for an expedition to Greece to measure exactly the Parthenon and other buildings. With the financial help of several wealthy members of the Society of Dilettanti (a club comprised of English veterans of the Grand Tour,[15] whose toast was "To Grecian Taste and Roman Spirit") Stuart and Revett finally reached Athens in March 1751. While Stuart made sketches of the buildings, Revett recorded the dimensions of every architectural detail, using "a Rod of Brass, three feet long, most accurately divided."

They finished in 1753, and after barely escaping with their lives, reached England in 1755. Following delays due both to careful preparation of the

[15] Lionel Cust, *A History of the Society of Dilettanti*, 1914.

plates and to Stuart's indolence, their superb elephant folio finally appeared
in 1762, with a dedication to the King, bearing the title, *The Antiquities of
Athens, Measured and Delineated*. Anticipation had been built up over so
many years (the proposals were issued in London in 1751 and in Venice in
1753) that publication was a major event. The list of subscribers reads like
a *Who's Who* of the world of taste, containing besides the aristocrats, Sir
Joshua Reynolds, David Garrick, Horace Walpole, Laurence Sterne, Ben-
jamin Franklin and the Abbé Barthélémy (of whom more in proper time).
Of equal significance, the leading men in the building trades had also subscribed their four guineas in advance. Stuart, now a famous man, was over-
whelmed with commissions and henceforth was known as "Athenian Stuart."
"Grecian Gusto" became the fashionable style in architecture both in Lon-
lications of other travellers. Only two months after they had begun work
don and the provinces. Ten years later the author of *Letters concerning the
Present State of England* reported:

> There is now a purity and Grecian elegance diffused through every part
> of the edifices erected in the present age; the ornaments of the ceilings,
> walls, and chimney-pieces, are in a stile unknown to the last age; instead
> of the heavy, clumsey exertions of blundering artists, whose utmost efforts
> of finery reached no higher than much gilding, we now see the choicest
> remnants of the finest ages of antiquity made the standard of our taste.
> The rooms fitted up from the designs of Mr. Stuart, have an elegance
> unrivaled in all the p[a]laces of Europe.[16]

Parenthetically it should be remarked that the Grecian style in the eighteenth century was primarily in decorative details; the Greek revival in
architectural structure did not occur until the nineteenth century. In point
of fact the second (1789) and third (1794) volumes of Stuart and Revett
first revealed the Doric style to the world in full detail.

In the interval between the issuing of Stuart and Revett's Proposals in
1748 and publication in 1762 the new taste had been furthered by the pub-
in Athens two Englishmen turned up, James Dawkins and Robert Wood,
on their way to Palmyra and Baalbec. When Wood's beautifully illustrated
Ruins of Palmyra or Tedmor in the Desart came out in 1753 it carried a
handsome compliment to Stuart and Revett that heightened eagerness
among those who had read their original proposals. Dawkins, the silent but
wealthy partner, subscribed for twenty copies of *The Antiquities of Athens*,
to follow his earlier help, for he had issued the 1751 London proposals.

---

[16] 1772, p 244–245.

Another traveller in Greece who had read the 1748 proposals was the Frenchman, Julien David LeRoy. LeRoy got to Greece in 1754, the year after Stuart and Revett had left, and on the basis that national honor was at stake with the help of friends at the French court managed to publish in 1758 *Les Ruines des plus beaux Monuments de la Grèce*. The book was warmly received and promptly translated into English (1759). Stuart and Revett were piqued because LeRoy nowhere mentioned them or their project, but particularly because he had tried to steal their market. Consequently, when the first volume of *The Antiquities of Athens* made its tardy

Stuart's drawing of the Erechtheum; at right he depicts himself at work.
James Stuart and Nicholas Revett, *Antiquities of Athens* (London 1762–1830) vol II ch 2 plate 2 detail

appearance in 1762, Stuart took pains to point out the mistakes in LeRoy's plates as well as the errors that LeRoy had taken over from Spon and Wheler. The controversy was not left unnoticed by reviewers, and the aspect of national rivalry added to the widening interest in Hellenic antiquities.

The Society of Dilettanti was so impressed with the value of Stuart and Revett's first volume that they decided to send out an expedition to measure and delineate antiquities in other parts of Greece. Revett agreed to go again to do the measuring, a youthful artist named William Pars was employed to sketch and paint, and for the learned descriptions they engaged on Robert Wood's recommendation Richard Chandler, a young Oxonian who had already earned a reputation in archaeography with *Marmora Oxonensia* (1763), a careful account of the specimens owned by the University, including those brought back by Sir George Wheler. The book produced by this team, *Ionian Antiquities: or Ruins of Magnificent and Famous Buildings in Ionia* (1769), lived up to the expected standards, combining the virtues that Revett had displayed in the 1762 *Athens* with the vivid detail of Spon and Wheler. Chandler followed with two volumes of excerpts from his journals, the first being *Travels in Asia Minor* (1775) and the second, *Travels in Greece* (1776). These volumes served as the well of knowledge about modern Greece for the next two generations.

The archaeographical phase of Neo-Hellenism had now reached its crest. Stuart became involved in politics with his patron, the Marquis of Rockingham, who gathered a group of aristocrats and gentlemen weekly at Stuart's house on Leicester Square. The professed purpose of these meetings was to discuss Greek literature and antiquities, though skeptics whispered that the business of the Rockingham party was the chief topic of conversation.

Stuart dawdled so long with the important second volume, showing the "Buildings erected while the Athenians were a free people," that at the time of his death in 1788, sixteen years after the first volume, it was not yet ready for publication, though his widow managed to put it into the hands of the public in the following year. The third volume followed in 1794 with a preface by Willey Revely, notable for its answer to the posthumous attack which Sir William Chambers, champion of the Vitruvian and Palladian schools of architecture, had made on Stuart. Chambers considered that the Parthenon appeared deformed by "gouty columns"; he stated that it was less attractive and smaller than the church of St Martin in the Fields, and that its appearance would be improved by the addition of a steeple! Revelly retorted that Chamber's ignorance of the Parthenon derived from his friend and correspondent LeRoy, that the Parthenon was about a third larger than St Martin in the Fields, and he asked why Sir Robert (author of a book on Chinoiserie) had not suggested adding a pagoda instead of a steeple? Revelly concluded, ". . . the popularity into which Grecian principles are daily growing, in spite of the feeble attempts that have been made to decry them, is the best answer to such undistinguishing assailants" (p 19–26). An unstated irony is that "Athenian" Stuart had been buried in St Martin in the Fields shortly before Chambers published his attack.

Remaining events in the archaeographic phase of the Greek Revival can be summarized briefly without the need for detailed comment. In 1806 the

Newdigate Poetry Prize at Oxford was first put on a regular footing; the chosen subject was "A Recommendation of the Study of the Remains of Ancient Grecian and Roman Architecture, Sculpture and Painting," and the contestants were restricted to only fifty lines of verse in covering this broad subject. The winner, a young Scot named John Wilson, survived to enjoy a literary career under the pseudonym of "Christopher North." The fourth and last volume of Stuart's *Antiquities of Athens* did not appear until 1816, edited by Joseph Woods, and consisting mainly of odds and ends from Stuart's papers, along with a biographical memoir.[17]

In the meantime, thanks to Lord Elgin's having in 1801 convinced the Sultan to allow Englishmen easy access to Greece, travellers began to come in droves. Thus Goethe, in setting the third act of the second part of *Faust* in Greece, has Mephistopheles ask the Sphinx,

> Are Britons here? So round the world they wheel,
> To stare at battlefields, historic traces,
> Cascades, old walls and classic dreary places;
> And here were something worthy of their zeal.[18]

By now the Greek war for independence was just around the corner, and when peace came, Prince Otho of Bavaria had been crowned King of the Hellenes and a century of German archaeology had begun.

Before leaving this scientific phase of Neo-Hellenism, a comment is in order concerning the state of Greek studies in England. Aside from the efforts of Richard Bentley, Greek scholarship lay quiescent. The universities remained in the state so well described by Gibbon, when the dons were "sunk in prejudice and port," and professorships were regarded as little more than livings. In 1779 when Andrew Dalzel was appointed to the Greek professorship at Edinburgh the status of his chair was at the lowest ebb. Philological studies were far behind archaeographical in concept: in 1783 when Richard Porson was invited by the Cambridge University Press to prepare a new text of Aeschylus and replied that the manuscript in the Laurentian Library at Florence should be collated, the syndics of the Press

---

[17] Beginning in 1810 classical topography became a popular branch of archaeography with Sir William Gell's *Itinerary of Greece*, a sub-genre that he exploited to the full. In 1812 William Wilkins, the future architect of Downing College, Cambridge, of University College, London, and the National Gallery, whose career is linked with the Greek Revival, published *Atheniensia, or Remarks on the Topography and Buildings of Athens*. Edward Dodwell's *Classical and Topographical Tour through Greece*, in two volumes quarto, followed in 1819. Two years earlier the Dilettanti Society had published an *omnium gatherum*, entitled *Unedited Antiquities of Attica*.

[18] From Bayard Taylor's translation, Act III scene i.

gravely suggested that "Mr. Porson might *collect* his manuscripts at home."[19]
A new era in Greek studies was clearly overdue. It began in 1793 when Porson was appointed Regius Professor at Cambridge.

Long before Neo-Hellenism reached its Romantic phase, romantic elements occurred abundantly in the early travel books. Indeed, the fictional Monsieur de la Guilletière set the tone in *Athènes ancienne et nouvelle* (1675) when he described his sentiments on approaching the city, a passage overlooked by writers on Romantic Hellenism:

> And here I cannot but acknowledge my own weakness, you may call it folly if you please: At the first sight of this Famous Town (struck as it were with a sentiment of Veneration for those Miracles of Antiquity which were Recorded of it) I started immediately, and was taken with an universal shivering all over my Body. Nor was I singular in my Commotion, we all of us stared, but could see nothing, our imaginations were too full of the Great Men which that City had produced. (p 123–124)

In turn, Spon and Wheler echoed this attitude, though with proper restraint. When the adolescent Aaron Hill reached Greece he "found a certain pleasure in the very looking at a Place of such *Antiquity*."

Lady Mary Wortley Montagu, equally moved, enshrined her sentiments in verse:

> Warm'd with poetic transport I survey
> Th' immortal islands, and the well-known sea;
> For here so oft the muse her heart has strung,
> And not a mountain rears his head unsung.[20]

From Troy she wrote to Alexander Pope, "I read over your Homer here with an infinite pleasure, and find several little passages explained, that I did not before entirely comprehend the beauty of." Pope responded, ". . . you may lay the immortal work on some broken column of a hero's sepulchre, and read the fall of Troy in the shade of a Trojan ruin." [21]

As the century progressed and romantic sentiments became more common the very word "Grecian" produced an emotional response in the minds of all who had read Homer, even Pope's translation into heroic couplets which Bentley had decried for its lack of Homeric quality. Like Pope, other writers who had not visited Greece in the flesh travelled there in spirit, and poured their emotional response into their writings. First (and least roman-

---

[19] J. E. Sandys, *History of Classical Scholarship* (1908) ii 427.
[20] *Letters and Works of Lady Mary Wortley Montagu* (1893) i 300.
[21] *Correspondence of Alexander Pope*, ed G. Sherburn (1956) i 440.

tic) is that strange Scotsman, Andrew Ramsay, who spent most of his life in France in the service of the exiled Stuarts, where he was known as Le Chevalier Ramsay. In 1727 Ramsay published *Les Voyages de Cyrus*, an imaginary account of the education of Cyrus, prince of Persia in the time of Xenophon, as he travelled with a philosophical tutor on a Grand Tour of the eastern Mediterranean. Book IV describes Cyrus's experiences in Greece, where Solon shows him around Athens, explains its laws and describes the life of the citizens. Cyrus is also taken to a performance at the theatre and given a lecture on Greek tragic drama. *Les Voyages de Cyrus* immediately became a best seller, and went through over thirty editions in English and French before the end of the century, not to mention translations into German, Italian, Spanish, and ultimately into modern Greek. Space does not permit detailed discussion of its content or influence, except to remark that it demonstrates the existence of a wide audience eager for information about life in antiquity. (Remember, the novel had not yet come into being, so travel books attracted readers hungry for narrative fiction.)

Perhaps the most lasting effect of Ramsay's *Les Voyages de Cyrus* was that it prepared the way for *Les Voyages du Jeune Anacharsis*, published after thirty years of incubation in 1789 by the Abbé Barthélémy. Although Barthélémy had traveled no farther than Rome, he was a keen student of Greek antiquity (we have noted earlier that he was a subscriber to Stuart's and Revett's *Antiquities of Athens*). Despite the fact that eight volumes were required to recount the *Travels of Anacharsis the Younger, in Greece*, ten editions were called for in the first ten years, not to mention translations into English and other languages, extending to Danish, Dutch, Armenian, and modern Greek. It tells how the young philosopher, Anacharsis, comes from Scythia to Greece in the middle of the fourth century and visits all the famous places. Anacharsis first learns about earlier events of Greek history. He then describes with proper romantic sentiments the appearance of Greek cities, temples, and statues; he inquires particularly into the laws and forms of government, and warms to the praise of democracy and the glorious state of liberty.

That publication of this book coincided with the dawn of the French Revolution accounts for some of its phenomenal success, and also for the enthusiasm with which the Revolutionists identified themselves with the ancient Greeks. Political leaders enjoyed comparing themselves with heroes of the age of Pericles, for democracy and liberty were now revived in Paris, along with other Athenian virtues. The women of fashion followed the

example, and modeled their dress on that of the ancient Greeks; they wore
sandals and tunics, cut their hair in imitation of statues or bound it with
fillets over which they wore hats constructed to look like classic helmets.
Carlyle's graphic description comes to mind, "Behold her, that beautiful
adventurous Citoyenne: in costume of the Ancient Greeks, such Greek as
Painter David could teach; her sweeping tresses snooded by glittering antique fillet; bright-dyed tunic of the Greek women; her little feet naked,
as in Antique Statues, with mere sandals, and winding-strings of riband —
defying the frost." [22] Barthélémy's *Travels of Anacharsis* was only one cause
behind this sentimental enthusiasm for ancient Greece, but the importance
of the book in the rise of Romantic Hellenism in Europe can scarcely be
exaggerated.

To return to Britons in Greece, one of the accidents of fate was the sur-
vival of a Scottish sailor named William Falconer when his ship went down
in a storm off the ruined temple on Cape Sunium, an experience which he
versified and published in 1762 as *The Shipwreck*. Present day literary historians look down their noses at Falconer's didactic verses, but they moved
a generation of readers, and influenced poems as recent as Masefield's
Dauber. Falconer contributed to the rising stream of Romantic Hellenism
by interrupting his narrative to describe the ruins of Greece in sentimental
terms, thus becoming the first traveller to do so in verse.

Surprisingly, the last quarter of the eighteenth century saw only a dozen
or so British travellers in "dry Greece," aside from the archaeographers
already mentioned and others on official missions. One of the most devout
was Thomas Watkins in 1788, who on landing at Piraeus kissed the classic
ground. In the meantime a controversy raged at home that involved
numerous Hellenists, the "Troy Controversy." In brief it concerned the
problem of locating the Homeric city, but expanded to the question of
whether the Trojan war was merely a creation of the poet's imagination.[23]
A dozen learned men published tracts or dissertations on the subject, the
academics' arguments being based on writings of the ancient geographers,
and the travellers' on their actual visits to the Troade. In 1804 Sir William
Gell settled the matter with his *Topography of Troy and its Vicinity*.

The year 1800 marks the beginning of another controversy, for in that
year another Scot, Thomas Bruce, seventh Earl of Elgin, having recently
been appointed (at the age of thirty-three) Ambassador to the Porte, sent

---

[22] *The French Revolution*, ed C. R. L. Fletcher (1902) III 223.
[23] M. L. Clarke, *Greek Studies in England, 1700–1830* (1945) 184 et passim.

before him a group of technicians to make plaster casts of statuary in "the Temple of the Idols" as the Turkish authorities called the Parthenon. The following year permission was granted "to take away any pieces of stone with old inscriptions or figures thereon." During the next two years Elgin's "predatory band" were busily at work, and included such distinguished visitors as his Lordship's father and mother-in-law and Dr Carlyle, Professor of Arabic at Cambridge. The story is well known of the transportation of the Elgin Marbles to London and of the long controversy over their merits, before Parliament in 1816 finally purchased them for the nation (at £35,000, less than half the amount Elgin had invested in them). The British public, stimulated by the controversy, flocked to see the sculptures. Whether the

Antiquities of Athens vol II ch 1 plate 30 detail

stones were authentic works of Phidias or were merely Roman copies became the foremost artistic issue of the day, and ultimately became a political issue as well, the Liberals taking the opposition. Once the marbles were ensconced in the British Museum they became the most popular exhibit, and we read that the cows of the Athenian hectacomb excited the admiration of English cattle breeders and that a riding master decided to bring his pupils to study the marbles in preference to giving them a riding lesson, so that they might contemplate for an hour these riders.[24] The glories of the Phidean school were now open for the eyes of all to see. The result was a revolution in taste; the delicate, polished style of the Hellenistic Venuses and Apollos (complete to their fingertips) was gradually replaced by the rough, energetic, fragmentary style of the age of Pericles. Ancient Greek art became established on the pinnacle already occupied by Greek philosophy and Greek poetry — the pinnacle of perfection beyond all emulation. Romantic Hellenism had reached its zenith.

So far there has been no occasion to mention Lord Byron. As we have seen, by 1810 the path up the Acropolis was well trodden by the boots of English travellers, most of whom wrote up their experiences in one form or another. Before the adolescent Byron entered Cambridge (1805) the public had received poetical descriptions of Greece written by Dr Carlyle (already

24 J. T. Smith, *Nollekens and His Times* (1829) chapter 11.

mentioned), including one titled "On Viewing Athens from the Pnyx, by the light of a waning moon." The bulk of the Elgin marbles had already arrived in London in 1804. Indeed, Byron took a reactionary attitude towards them, and before he set out for Greece in 1809 condemned them as "freaks . . . misshappen monuments and maim'd antiques . . . mutilated blocks of art." [25]

A few months before Byron left England he read a book of poems entitled *Horae Ionicae* written by W. R. Wright, sometime Consul General of the Ionian Isles. Greatly impressed, he inserted a passage praising the book into *English Bards and Scotch Reviewers:*

> . . . doubly blest is he whose heart expands
> With hallowed feelings for those classic lands.
> Who rends the veil of ages long gone by,
> And views the remnants with a poet's eye!
> WRIGHT! 'Twas thy happy lot at once to view
> Those shores of glory, and to sing them too;
> And sure no common Muse inspired thy pen
> To hail the land of Gods and Godlike men.
>   (lines 873–880)

Here, indeed, was a program for Byron to follow; to write not another travel book in prose (that task was left to his companion, Hobhouse [26]) but to write poetical travels centering on a fictional character. Thus when the first two books of *Childe Harold's Pilgrimage* were published in March 1812, the world welcomed it as a poetical travel book by a new major poet. But when the Grecian canto (the second) is read with the earlier travel books and poems in mind, we see that Byron had little new to say, regardless of the emotional and poetic power with which he said it. The Greek canto begins by lashing his whipping boy, Lord Elgin, then, after taking us to Albania, Istanbul, and the Bosphorus, returns to wallop the despoilers of Greek statuary. Childe Harold does not reach Greece proper until the 73d stanza, so that only a third of the canto is actually given to Greece. The principal idea expressed by Byron's "gloomy wanderer" is a lament on the old theme of lost liberty; the modern Greeks he considered "a degenerated horde," "From birth to death enslaved; in word, in deed, unmann'd." There are even

[25] *English Bards and Scotch Reviewers,* lines 1027–32. In 1810, visiting the Acropolis daily, he came to take a different view. "These relics that were being carried away were not now in his eyes worthless stones . . . but the heritage of the finest culture of the Greek race. . . ." Leslie A. Marchand, *Byron* (1957) I 224–225.

[26] Hobhouse carried a large supply of paper and ink, as well as the standard books on Greece. He would spend his mornings studying the classic sites while Byron was poetizing, and then take Byron back to the site in the afternoon. Hobhouse's *Journey through Albania* was published in 1813. See Marchand I 266, 268, III 1107, 1115–16.

indications that at this time Byron preferred the Turks to the Greeks, an attitude common among English merchants in the Levant.[27]

During the next ten years Byron returned again and again to Greek scenes for his poems. Like other writers of travel books, histories, and poems he ranged beyond Greece to other areas of the Levant, for the whole Near East had become popular subject matter. W. C. Brown who studied "The Popularity of English Travel Books about the Near East, 1775–1825," [28] has supplied impressive evidence, especially from contemporary magazines, remarking, "It is hardly possible to open a single issue of a periodical of the time without encountering a review or a listing of some new travel account of the Near East" (p 74). His subsequent study of minor poetry of the same fifty years led to the following conclusions:

> First, the application of these contemporary ideas to the Near East obviously originated in the travel books. Second, the popularity of the travel-book material made these themes easily accessible to the minor poets at home. Third . . . the minor poets not only read extensively in the travel books, but . . . appropriated the travellers' dominant ideas. Finally, by so doing the minor poets helped to reinforce the vogue of these ideas in England and the association of them with the Near East. Thus the minor poetry, as well as the travel books, played an important part in creating the milieu of English interest in the Near East.[29]

Of all the areas in the Near East it was Greece, of course, that excited the most emotion.

As noted earlier, the French were second only to the British in producing travel books about Greece. Pierre Guys set the tone with his *Voyage Littéraire de la Grèce* in 1771, which promptly appeared in an English translation with the Sternian title, *A Sentimental Journey Through Greece*. These books, like the *Travels of Anacharsis* already mentioned, were widely circulated in England. Byron, a voracious reader, had gulped down the literature of Near Eastern travel from boyhood on. He scribbled, "Knolles, Cantemir, De Tott, Lady M. W. Montagu, Hawkins's translation from Mignot's History of the Turks, the Arabian Nights — all travels or histories, or books upon the East, I could meet with, I had read, as well as Ricaut, before I was ten years old." [30]

---

[27] See his letter of 3 May 1810: "I see not much difference between ourselves and the Turks. . . . I like the Greeks, who are plausible rascals, — with all the Turkish vices, without their courage." But he was superior to, and amused by, the merchants' contempt of those they exploited. See Marchand i 226 and Byron's note on stanza 73.

[28] *Philological Quarterly* xv (Jan 1936) 70–80.

[29] *Philological Quarterly* xvi (July 1937) 271.

[30] Moore's *Life of Byron* (1830) i 255.

The idea that the Greeks should once again become free goes back at least to the early seventeenth century. Terence Spencer has chronicled the subject so thoroughly that here a nutshell summary will suffice. In short, after 1687 when the Venetians briefly occupied Athens and the Peloponnesus, the population began to be stirred from the hopeless state they had known for two hundred years. In 1770 an abortive revolt occurred inspired by Catherine of Russia, which drew world wide attention to Greece. By the 1790s Turkey was recognized as the "sick man of Europe" and the great powers — Russia, Britain, and Napoleonic France — each feared that the others might take advantage of the situation. The emergence of a modern Greek literary revival led by Rhegas (d.1798) crystallized nationalist sentiment, and simultaneously the "fallout" of the French Revolution carried to distant lands. The revolt of Byron's friend the Ali Pasha of Albania in 1820 touched off the action in Greece proper. Once it had begun, the interests of the Great Powers, however tardy in participation, made the outcome certain.

Byron, in the meantime, followed the shift in attitude towards the Greek people, albeit somewhat belatedly. In the eyes of all Europe he had become the image of the Philhellene; thus an inevitability of fate called him to join in the cause with which, somewhat paradoxically, he was identified. Sir Harold Nicholson in *Byron: the Last Journey* has described in detail the personal factors in his decision and the magnificent courage he displayed during the nine months before his death at Missolonghi. From that day onward travel books had a new tone, for Philhellenism, especially fascination with the birth of a new nation that had won liberty on classic ground where liberty (according to accepted myth) first grew, now reached its crest. Of course, the romantic tone persisted, and archaeography also, though it became transposed to archaeology as digging became a science, especially after the Germans (to the annoyance of the British) took over under the patronage of King Otho.

Once peace broke out Greece became for the prosperous British a popular extension of the Grand Tour. Athens was now as accessible as Avignon had been a few generations earlier. Journals, diaries, and other travel books proliferated from the pens of the classical Dr Syntaxes who set out "to make a tour and write it." The successful development of the steam printing press drastically reduced publishing costs; so travel books along with all others poured forth in an expanding flood.

Only a few events remain to be mentioned. First, let us salute a milestone in the annals of the travel industry: in April of 1833, less than a year after Otho had been crowned, the first organized cruise ship, the SS *Francois*

Premier, sailed for Greece. The passenger list signifies the importance of this enterprise, for it includes several ambassadors, the brother of King Otho, Madame la Duchesse de Berry, and, as might be expected, sundry English travellers.[31]

A second event, equally notable as a portent of a whole future industry, was the publication in 1840 of Murray's *Handbook for Travellers in the Ionian Isles, Greece,* etc. Ostensibly this should have eliminated the need for further travel books, but no change in the output can be noted. Actually, so many tourists were crawling over the Greek landscape, a writer in the *Quarterly Review* in 1842 complained, that Greece was being westernized and romance had gone out of the Hellenic pilgrimage.[32] Only four years later, in 1846, Thackeray found his visit to Athens a subject ripe for satire in his burlesque of travel books, *Notes of a Journey from Cornhill to Grand Cairo by Michel Angelo Titmarsh:*

> Not feeling any enthusiasm myself about Athens, my bounden duty of course is clear, to sneer and laugh heartily at all who have. . . . What call have young ladies to consider Greece "romantic" — they who get their notions of mythology from the well-known pages of Tooke's *Pantheon?* What is the reason that blundering Yorkshire squires, young dandies from Corfu regiments, jolly sailors from ships in the harbour, and yellow old Indians from Bundelcund, should think proper to be enthusiastic about a country of which they know nothing; the physical beauty of which they cannot, for the most part, comprehend; and because certain characters lived in it two thousand four hundred years ago? What have these people in common with Pericles, what have these ladies in common with Aspasia (O fie)? Of the race of Englishmen who come wandering about the tomb of Socrates, do you think the majority would not have voted to hemlock him? Yes; for the very same superstition which leads men by the nose now, drove them onward in the days when the lowly husband of Xantippe died for daring to think simply and to speak the truth.[33]

By this time the scribbling travellers had done their work, and Philhellenism had grown beyond the measuring and delineating into an understanding of the principles of Greek architecture and how they could be used in northern Europe. Similarly, classical scholars who had visited Greece were illuminating the texts and the literature. Grote and Finlay were writing the history

[31] Two printed accounts exist in the Gennadius Library at Athens, and doubtless elsewhere; the first by J. Girandeau (1835) and the second by someone who wrote under the pseudonym, Marchebeus (1839).

[32] *Quarterly Review* LXXX No. cxxxix 130–131.

[33] *Burlesques; From Cornhill to Grand Cairo* (1903) 271.

of Greece with authority, especially Finlay, who invested his inherited capital in Greek real estate and penned his pages in the ashes of disillusionment.

Thus Neo-Hellenism can be seen as a phenomenon, in both intellectual history and the history of taste, that passed through several phases. Just as reading of the classics had prepared earlier generations to think of Greece as the homeland of the greatest poets and philosophers, so the books written by successive generations of travellers — once such travel became possible — prepared the public for successive new attitudes towards things Greek. In a nation where prose fiction commonly utilized travel plots and situations (*Robinson Crusoe, Gulliver, Tom Jones, Humphrey Clinker, Rasselas,* etc, etc) it is not surprising that travel books rivalled fiction in popularity, as library records show.[34] Indeed, the books by travellers to Greece prepared the audience for *Childe Harold's Pilgrimage,* itself in turn a travel book that created a wave of sympathy for Greece just before the struggle for independence.

Before the nineteenth century had ended, Neo-Hellenism passed into a new phase. The romantic view became superseded by a relatively clear-eyed objectivity, based on scholarship. The emotion-charged image of Greece became transformed into a rational understanding of actualities. (Emotional attitudes towards Greece will, of course, persist, but the actualities have become available for those who wish to know them.) With the founding of the British School in Athens in 1886, British archaeologists began to regain their laurels usurped by the Germans. And with Arnold, Jebb, Jowett, Gilbert Murray, and others, Hellenism became a vital factor in English culture. The "Greek way of life" came to be a phrase spoken with comprehension and conviction.

34 See below, pages 53–54.

Patrick Brydone

The Eighteenth-Century Traveler as Representative Man

By PAUL FUSSELL, JR

Rutgers University

ALTHOUGH the year 1773 was probably satisfactory for the London booksellers, it was hardly an *annus mirabilis* for literature. If one of the publishing events of the season was *She Stoops to Conquer,* another was the *Poems* of Mrs Anna Letitia Barbauld. Johnson brought out nothing during the year but a revision of the *Dictionary*; he left it to Lord Monboddo to speculate in print about *The Origin and Progress of Language.* The reader of taste must have thought it a barren season, and, although he could console himself by bringing home the ten volumes of George Steevens' new edition of Shakespeare, he may be forgiven if he thirsted also for some satisfying writing by contemporaries.

In the absence of more splendid matter, many readers in this year betook themselves to volumes of travel, and of the year's travel books two became conspicuously popular. One is John Hawkesworth's *An Account of the Voyages . . . for Making Discoveries in the Southern Hemisphere* (3 vols). Perhaps the most appealing part of this book is the account of Captain James Cook's explorations in the bark *Endeavour* of "Otaheite" and adjacent islands, a subject clearly exotic enough to appeal widely. The other travel book, which seems at first less promising, is Patrick Brydone's *A Tour through Sicily and Malta. In a Series of Letters to William Beckford, Esq. of Somerly in Suffolk* (2 vols).

The borrowing records of the Bristol Library, the only such eighteenth-century records yet uncovered, indicate that Brydone's *Tour* was in great demand. In fact, it proves to be the third most popular item with borrowers in Bristol for the two years following publication, and during the next eleven years it became the second most popular. During the period 1773–1775, Hawkesworth's *Voyages* was borrowed 115 times, Chesterfield's *Letters* (1774) 104 times, and Brydone's *Tour* 100 times; and during the eleven years from 1773 to 1784 the only book in greater demand than Brydone's was Hawkesworth's. Over the long, eleven-year run, Chesterfield's *Letters* sank to third place. Fourth was Hume's *History of England,* and fifth was Goldsmith's *History of the Earth and of Animated Nature.* The runners-up were two more histories, Guillaume Raynal's *History of the Settlements and Trade of the Europeans in the East and West Indies* (trans J. Justamond) and William Robertson's *History of the Reign of the Emperor Charles V.* We encounter works of fiction only near the bottom of the list of the ten most popular books during this eleven-year period: *Tristram Shandy* is in eighth place, and Fielding's *Works* is last, just below Lord Lyttelton's *History of the Life of King Henry the Second.*[1] Even when we consider that library borrowings do not constitute very substantial evidence — books are often borrowed for ostentation rather than use, and many books are too popular even to be stocked by libraries — statistics such as these seem at least suggestive of certain tendencies of taste.

Unless we are reminded by some such indication as this, we may tend to forget that throughout the eighteenth century the travel book was one of the primary genres, and one so appealing in its focus and conventions that almost every writer of consequence worked in the form, from Defoe and Addison to Fielding, Smollett, Boswell, Johnson, and Sterne. And it is obvious that countless works of a more overtly fictional cast tended to ape the travel book, from *Gulliver's Travels* to *Rasselas* and — to stretch the boundaries a bit — *Childe Harold's Pilgrimage.* In poetry the immense vogue of the "excursion poem"[2] — Goldsmith titled his exercise in the form *The Traveller* — reflects the appeal of the prose "kind" which is its ancestor and analogue. Pope's invitation to Bolingbroke to "expatiate free o'er all this scene of man" enacts the prime intellectual invitation of contemporary travel literature. When the twenty-three-year-old Wordsworth wanted to appear in print poetically, it was natural that he do so under the title *Descriptive Sketches Taken During a Pedestrian Tour Among the Alps* (1793): an audience for tours, whether couched in Brydone's prose "letters" or in Wordsworth's heroic couplets, was both abundant and willing to be pleased. It was largely the same audience which sustained the vogue of the picaresque in the novel. Indeed, the eighteenth-century literature we know would hardly be recognizable if we subtracted from it all its prevailing images of a rational and sturdy observer wandering about foreign parts, collecting data, patronizing the natives — or, if they are Swiss, flattering them — and reporting his findings for the benefit of stay-at-homes. These presiding images derive not only from such real personages as Samuel Johnson in the Hebrides and James Boswell on the Grand Tour, but also from a host of fictive counterparts so various as Gulliver, Lien Chi Altangi, and the young Simkin Blunderhead of *The New Bath Guide.* There is something about both the actual experience of travel and

---

[1] Paul Kaufman, *Borrowings from the Bristol Library: 1773–1784* (Charlottesville 1960) 122.
[2] See Marjorie Hope Nicolson, *Mountain Gloom and Mountain Glory: The Development of the Aesthetics of the Infinite* (Ithaca 1959) 329 ff.

the literary experience of the travel report, whether straight, ironic, or "sentimental," that comes very near the heart of the dominant eighteenth-century idea of knowledge as a sequential accumulation of particulars collected from a multifarious but verifiable objective reality. The contemporary plausibility of Lockean psychology thus provides the context for appreciating the vigor of the travel book as one of the most flourishing eighteenth-century kinds. As Jean H. Hagstrum has observed, "If one is . . . committed to outside reality rather than to introspection, it becomes even more necessary to vary that reality by travel and by the extended observation that it provides." [3]

Of the author of the amazingly popular *Tour through Sicily and Malta* not a great deal is to be discovered.[4] Patrick Brydone was a lowland Scot, born in 1736 somewhere in Berwickshire. We hear of his matriculating at St Andrew's in 1750–1751 as one of the students of Walter Wilson, Professor of Greek. That he was later delighted to have had the classics poured into him is apparent on almost every page of the *Tour*, where names like Diodorus Siculus and Apollonius Rhodius drop like rain. After the university he apparently served in the Army as a captain. That he was a Freemason is attested in the *Tour* (II 45).[5] As a young man he was devoted to electricity — a passion he never lost — and he once traveled through the Alps conducting electrical experiments. It was perhaps here that he developed the fascination with mountains which appears in the *Tour*. We hear of him abroad again around 1768, when he traveled as tutor to a young man, one William Beckford of Suffolk, who is not to be confused with the author of *Vathek*. In 1770 he took the tour of Sicily and Malta recorded in the work of 1773. Around the time of the publication of the *Tour* he was elected Fellow of the Royal Society, and later he became a Fellow of both the Royal Society of Edinburgh and the Society of Antiquaries. Horace Walpole, who encountered him at a party in 1780, seems to have thought him a pushy Scot, ambitious for a place under Lord North.[6] Brydone evidently made some impression on the North ministry, for he did serve briefly as Comptroller of the Stamp Office. He retired to Berwickshire and died there in 1818. Except for some papers on electrical experiments published in the *Transactions of the Royal Society*, the *Tour through Sicily and Malta* is the only work he left behind. In its own day it was not only widely popular but critically successful.

[3] "Some Opportunities for Research in Eighteenth Century Literature," *Newberry Library Bulletin* III (1954) 180.

[4] The brief account in *DNB* is not to be trusted.

[5] I quote throughout from the two-volume edition of 1775 (London: Strahan and Cadell). The title-page of the first volume is a cancel.

[6] Letter to the Countess of Upper Ossory, Oct 10 1780.

Ralph Griffiths, who devoted two pieces in the *Monthly Review* to the *Tour* when it first appeared, said of Brydone that "[his] letters prove him at once the gentleman, the scholar, and the man of science: a rational observer, a philosophical enquirer, and a polite and pleasing companion." He concluded: "Captain Brydone's Tour contains more good sense, more knowledge, more variety of entertainment, than is to be found in *most* works of the kind: — in truth, we cannot, at present, recollect *one* that can be put in competition with it." [7] Boswell, whose *Corsica* had enjoyed a brisk circulation five years earlier, cannot have been comforted by Griffiths' italics; nor can he have been pleased to hear Johnson, discoursing to The Literary Club in 1775, assign Brydone's *Tour* the same eminence at the head of performances of its literary kind.[8] But even Boswell found the book "entertaining," like the numerous readers both common and sophisticated who consumed four separate editions during the three years following publication. Paul Franklin Kirby observes: "Brydone did for Sicily in the second half of the eighteenth century what Boswell did for Corsica. . . . Brydone's book seems to have become such a familiar part of the general reader's library that in 1776 when John Dryden Jr's *A Voyage to Sicily and Malta* was published posthumously, the printer thought it would promote sales to make it uniform with Brydone's volumes." [9]

Brydone was accompanied on his tour by the seventeen-year-old William Fullarton (later Colonel and Commissioner of Trinidad), by another friend named Glover, and by several servants. The journey was a rugged one. Indeed, before they started some of their Neapolitan friends told them it was impossible, pointing out that "there are no inns in the island, and [that] many of the roads are over dangerous precipices, or through bogs and forests, infested with the most resolute and daring banditti in Europe" (12). Thomas Nugent's famous *The Grand Tour* (4 vols 1749), one of the standard guidebooks of the day, conducts the traveler only as far as Messina, naturally assuming that no one will want to venture beyond. Undaunted, the travelers set out from Naples in the middle of May 1770 and proceeded by British ship to Messina, where they began their clockwise circuit of Sicily. First, holding aloft umbrellas to repel the heat, they rode by mule train to Giardina and Taormina. The next stop was Catania, where they undertook a rigorous two-day climb of Etna. Then a felucca took them to Syracuse; they were distressed to find the city in a condition of frightful squalor. Reaching

[7] *Monthly Review* XLIX (1773) 22; 121.
[8] *Life of Johnson,* April 7 1775.
[9] *The Grand Tour in Italy (1700–1800)* (Siena 1952) 164.

Capo Passero by boat, they endured a long wait for favorable weather before embarking on the 100-mile voyage to Malta, which they found delightfully romantic and unreal. They returned to Ragusa and spent some time exploring the Greek ruins at Agrigento, where they were painfully impressed by the contrast between the brilliant reputation of the ancient city and the poverty and superstition of the modern town. Taking a mule train across the island, they arrived at Palermo, which delighted them so much that they remained to observe the gaudy festival of St Rosalia (July 11–15) before returning by ship to Naples around the first of August 1770.

The four-month trip Brydone records in thirty-eight "letters" to Beckford, the kind of letters which had long stood as a favored vehicle for travel accounts. That Brydone is sensitive to the different conventions of the various prose genres seems apparent from his remarking at Catania: "I should not finish this account of mount Ætna, without saying something of the various fables and allegories to which it has given rise; but it would probably . . . give this more the air of a dissertation than a letter or a journal" (i 265). The "air" that he is seeking, on the other hand, is that of gentlemanly negligence; as he asks the reader to believe, "When I have nothing else to do, I generally take up the pen" (ii 36). But the illusion of negligence is transmitted less by the expression, which is forceful and lively, than by the loose structure and the frequent divagations into elegiac and skeptical themes, and into popular science, vulcanology, and aesthetics.

II

Perhaps one cause of the popularity of Brydone's *Tour* is its satisfaction of the contemporary audience's appetite for the elegiac. The tendency of much of the literature of the second half of the eighteenth century to turn in an elegiac direction is obvious: we think not only of Collins and Gray, but of Johnson regretting Dr Levet; of Gibbon recording the sad dissolution of the Roman empire and memorializing Julian the Apostate; of Burke mourning the death of European chivalry and remembering Marie Antoinette. The dark sense of mutability and loss is a primary constituent of the later eighteenth-century consciousness. Both Richard West and the splendors and heroisms of antiquity are gone, and their loss can never be supplied. It is instructive that many of Johnson's most memorable phrasings issue from elegiac occasions; Garrick's death, for example, "has eclipsed the gaiety of nations." Brydone's *Tour* exploits the sites of antique glory as pretexts for elegiac moralizing in the tradition of Dyer's *Ruins of Rome* (1740), a vital tradition up through Shelley's "Ozymandias" (1818). Ruminating on the ruins like Shelley's "traveller from an antique land," Dyer is moved to moralize:

> Vain end of human strength, of human skill,
> Conquest, and triumph, and domain, and pomp . . .

Brydone likewise delights to contemplate the mutabilities, losses, and vanities; reminding us of the Gibbon of 1764 contemplating "the barefooted friars . . . singing vespers in the temple of Jupiter," he writes:

> This delightful coast [south of Naples], once the garden of all Italy, and inhabited only by the rich, the gay, and luxurious, is now abandoned to the poorest and most miserable of mortals. Perhaps, there is no spot on the globe, that has undergone so thorough a change; or that can exhibit so striking a picture of the vanity of human grandeur.   (I 14)

And he adds that he and his friends went porcupine shooting "on the Monte Barbaro, the place that formerly produced the Falernian wine, but now a barren waste" (I 15–16). Again, the squalor of contemporary Syracuse, "now reduced to a heap of rubbish," moves Brydone to recall its condition in antiquity, renowned for "glory, magnificence, and illustrious deeds both in arts and arms" (I 287). With what pleasing melancholy he observes that many of the modern Syracusans are "over-run with the itch" (I 309). The acceptability of Brydone's presentation of decayed classical grandeur — together with his cheerful satire on religious superstition — helps explain the readiness, three years later, of Gibbon's audience. Gibbon was not the only one to find significance in declines and falls, nor to salt his prolonged elegy with skeptical asides.

In the *Reflections on the Revolution in France,* Burke inquires: "Who now reads Bolingbroke? Who ever read him through?" Although Burke and his friends were not reading Bolingbroke in 1790, Brydone and many others were apparently reading him in 1773. Listing "many of our celebrated poets and philosophers," Brydone speaks of Bacon, Shakespeare, Milton, Dryden, Pope, and Bolingbroke (II 316). One of the important themes of Brydone's *Tour* is the triumph of science over superstition. Readers of both Brydone and Gibbon found enough wry skepticism to gratify their taste, and like Gibbon, Brydone is sometimes coy; at Agrigento, musing on his discovery of seashells on the top of a mountain, he enacts this comedy: "Now, the deluge recorded in Scripture, will hardly account for all the appearances of this sort to be met with, almost in every country in the world. — But I am interrupted by visitors; . . . Adieu" (II 19). The mock-interruption is Brydone's equivalent of the armor of irony in Gibbon's fifteenth and sixteenth chapters of the *Decline and Fall*. The gentle collision between British scientism and Mediterranean superstition Brydone sets forth with his customary brilliance: he informs us that the amber found in the mouth of the Giarretta River, formerly the classical Simetus, is collected by the natives and brought to Catania,

> where it is manufactured into the form of crosses, beads, saints, &c. and is sold at high prices to the superstitious people on the continent. We bought several of these respectable figures, and found them electrical in a high degree; powerfully attracting feathers, straws, and other light bodies; somewhat emblematical, you will say, of what they represent. — Some pieces of this amber contain flies and other insects curiously preserved in its substance; and we were not a little entertained with the ingenuity of one of the artists, who has left a large blue-bottle-fly, with its wings expanded, exactly over the head of a saint, to represent, he told us, *lo spirito santo* descending upon him.   (I 282–283)

Again, it is easy to sense the satisfaction with which Brydone's readers lingered over his description of some cloistered nuns at Messina: ". . . none of them had sincerity enough . . . to acknowledge the unhappiness of their situation. All pretended to be happy and contented. . . . However, some of them had a soft melancholy in their countenances, that gave the lie to their words . . ." (I 61). Brydone's interest in volcanos sometimes hastens him into more dangerously heretical courses. At one point, conjecturing that Etna has been erupting for at least 14,000 years, he recounts the difficulties encountered by one Signor Recupero, a local priest, who, in trying to write the natural history of Etna, has found "That Moses hangs like a dead weight upon him, and blunts all his zeal for inquiry. . . . The bishop, who is strenuously orthodox . . . has already warned him to be upon his guard, and not to pretend to be a better natural historian than Moses" (I 141–142). It is this passage that Johnson had in mind when, meeting Brydone's traveling companion Fullarton in 1778, he told him, "If Brydone were more attentive to his Bible, he would be a good traveller." [10] Boswell was another who sought comfort in a "full refutation" of the implications of Brydone's passage; he says that at Lichfield in 1776,

> Mr. [Thomas] Seward mentioned to us the observations which he had made upon the strata of earth in volcanos, from which it appeared, that they were so very different in depth at different periods, that no calculation whatever could be made as to the time required for their formation. This fully refuted an antimosaical remark introduced into Captain Bry-

[10] *Life of Johnson*, May 17 1778.

done's entertaining Tour, I hope heedlessly, from a kind of vanity which is too common in those who have not sufficiently studied the most important of all subjects. Dr. Johnson, indeed, had said before, independent of this observation, 'Shall all the accumulated evidence of the history of the world; — shall the authority of what is unquestionably the most ancient writing, be overturned by an uncertain remark such as this?" [11]

But even Brydone seems to have weakened after a few weeks in Sicily as he witnessed the gay devotional processions and saw how they diffused happiness in the form of balls, fireworks, and late collations. Delighted by the warmth and affection apparent at the Feast of St Rosalia in Palermo, he writes: ". . . if superstition often produces such effects, I sincerely wish we had a little more of it amongst us. I could have thrown myself down before St. Rosolia [*sic*], and blessed her for making so many people happy" (II 218).

But occasional momentary backslidings like this do not distract Brydone from his primary orientation as scientific observer and reporter. He wants to "account" for things, and he finds that one of the great defects of the Italian character is that "the people here seldom think of accounting for any thing" (I 9). His pleasure in scientific speculation appears throughout. He is devoted to recording thermometer and barometer readings. He speculates at length on the theory of comets (II 140–165). He recommends the wearing of "a waistcoat of the finest flannel . . . covered by another of the same size of silk" to produce by friction "a kind of electric atmosphere around the body, that might possibly be one of the best preservatives against the effect of damps" (I 239). He suggests that ladies given to wearing long, erect hairpins or wire capframes should "ground" themselves during thunderstorms with "a small chain or wire" leading from their heads to the floor (I 241–242). His barometric findings cause him to wonder whether childbirth is not easier at sea-level and in warm climates (II 80–81). But his triumph in this line is his project for increasing the destructive potential of an infantry battalion: each man, he proposes, should carry a small mirror as part of his kit; thus on sunny days distant targets could be set afire by the convergence of the reflections (I 306–308). If we are reminded of the projectors of The Grand Academy of Lagado, on the one hand, and of Bouvard and Pécuchet, on the other, we also think of Samuel Johnson mysteriously drying his scraped orange peelings, or measuring his cut fingernails to calculate their rate of growth.[12]

[11] *Ibid*, March 24 1776.
[12] *Ibid*, April 1 1775; Sept 9 1779.

But it is volcanos that most profoundly stimulate Brydone's scientific curiosity. The discovery of the ruins of Herculaneum in 1719 and of Pompeii in 1748, not to mention the Lisbon earthquake of 1755, had focussed attention on such second causes of the Sublime as volcanos, mountains, and earthquakes, although as early as 1704 John Dennis, in *The Grounds of Criticism in Poetry*, had asserted that the emotion of the Sublime is generated by volcanos, as well as by witchcraft, monsters, prodigies, and lions and tigers. And since at least 1728, when David Mallet published *The Excursion*, science and sublimity had sorted together in the descriptive poem devoted to such phenomena as thunderstorms, earthquakes, and volcanos.[13] Although it is scientific curiosity that impels Brydone's trip up Etna, what takes place during the expedition is less a scientific inquiry than a series of exercises in the experience of the Sublime. Writing of the climb up the mountain, he says that his party went "Sometimes through gloomy forests, which by daylight were delightful; but now, from the universal darkness, the rustling of the trees; the heavy, dull, bellowing of the mountain; the vast expanse of ocean stretched at an immense distance below us; inspired a kind of awful horror" (i 194–195). The appearance here of Pope's "universal darkness," from the last line of the *Dunciad*, suggests the literary sophistication with which Brydone is working all this up. He is entirely aware of what his audience wants, and he is at pains less to recount his experiences than to purvey the delight of literary recognition. Once arrived at the summit of Etna, he performs a juxtaposition of the Sublime and the scientific, implicit in empirical and associational theories of the Sublime, theories in which a naturalistic cause is always advanced for a Sublime effect. From the summit, he says, he saw "the most wonderful and most sublime sight in nature." Indeed, "no imagination has dared to form an idea of so glorious and so magnificent a scene." *Genesis, Paradise Lost*, and the end of the *Dunciad* are assumed to be in the reader's mind as Brydone continues: "Both sea and land looked dark and confused, as if only emerging from their original chaos; and light and darkness seemed still undivided. . . ." As the sun, "like the great Creator," rises to indicate the division of sea from land, "All appears enchantment," for "The senses unaccustomed to the sublimity of such a scene, are bewildered and confounded." [14] But after this performance, Brydone proceeds busily to advance scientific explanations for these phe-

---

[13] Nicolson 339–340.

[14] Creation imagery was conventional in contexts aspiring to the Sublime: Genesis i:3 is one of the examples used by Longinus (*On the Sublime* ix 9). See Thomas R. Edwards, Jr, "Light and Nature: A Reading of the *Dunciad*," PQ xxxix (1960) 452, n 9, and passim.

nomena: for example, the illusion of the reduction of distances, by which far points on Sicily appear nearby, Brydone is at pains to understand scientifically: "Perhaps this singular effect is produced by the rays of light passing from a rarer medium into a denser; which (from a well known law in optics) to an observer in the rare medium, appears to lift up the objects that are at the bottom of the dense one; as a piece of money placed in a bason appears lifted up as soon as the bason is filled with water" (I 202–207). Brydone's many scientifically curious readers felt no incongruity here: the rapid passage from splendid images of the Creation to "a piece of money placed in a bason," far from striking them as an illustration of the art of sinking in prose, they found natural and hence delightful. Thomson's *Seasons*, after all, had entirely accustomed them to thinking of the Sublime in connection with Newton's theories of optics.

In the same way, it is likely that Brydone's aesthetic assumptions reflect those of his audience and thus stand as a useful index of popular taste in the 1770s. In gardening, he stands with Addison, Pope, Shenstone, and William Mason in contemning topiary sculpture on the French model (I 147). A certain aesthetic primitivism, as well as a prefiguring of Coleridge's and Hazlitt's sense of "keeping," [15] lies behind his delicately wrought description of an evening during the boat trip from Capo Passero to Malta:

> The coast of Sicily began to recede; and in a short time, we found ourselves in the ocean. There was a profound silence, except the noise of the waves breaking on the distant shore, which only served to render it more solemn. It was a dead calm, and the moon shone bright on the waters. The waves from the late storm, were still high; but smooth and even, and followed one another with a slow and equal pace. The scene had naturally sunk us into meditation; we had remained near an hour without speaking a word, when our sailors began their midnight hymn to the Virgin. The music was simple, solemn, and melancholy, and in perfect harmony with the scene, and with all our feelings. They beat exact time with their oars, and observed the harmony and the cadence with the utmost precision. We listened with infinite pleasure to this melancholy concert, and felt the vanity of operas and oratorios.   (I 330–331)

Despite Brydone's final compulsion to moralize the episode, it is superbly rendered. We sense the tone of "Calm is All Nature Like a Resting Wheel" or "Lines Written Near Richmond, Upon the Thames, At Evening," poems on which Wordsworth was working only about fifteen years after the appearance of Brydone's book. Brydone is obviously a proficient in Burke's Beautiful as well as in Burke's Sublime.

[15] Cf *Biographia Literaria*, "Satyrane's Letters," Letter III; and *Lectures on the English Comic Writers*, passim.

That Brydone was aware that his audience shared his disgust for "false wit" we can deduce from his treatment of one of the sights of Palermo, the estate of the prince of Palagonia. This man, reports Brydone, "has devoted his whole life to the study of monsters and chimeras, greater and more ridiculous than ever entered into the imagination of the wildest writers of romance or knight-errantry." The prince's house is surrounded by 600 grotesque statues, and "of all that immense group, there is not one made to represent any object in nature." He proceeds: "It would require a volume to describe the whole, and a sad volume indeed it would make. He has put the heads of men to the bodies of every sort of animal, and the heads of every other animal to the bodies of men. . . . This is a strange species of madness; and it is truly unaccountable that he has not been shut up many years ago." His "phrenzy," however, has the social merit of employing many sculptors, and his statues seem to cause active damage only when pregnant women gaze at them; in fact, "several living monsters [have] been brought forth in the neighborhood" (ɪɪ 94–103). It is clear that the premises of simplicity and the probable underlie Brydone's aesthetic responses; his aesthetic observations in the *Tour* seem to assume that his common readers are conservative in these matters, preferring Gray's *Elegy*, for example, to Gray's Pindarics.

We can get a sense of Brydone's public too from observing his treatment of classical quotations. Sometimes in quoting the *Aeneid* he uses the translation by Christopher Pitt, and in quoting Homer he has recourse to Pope. His practice when he must give the original is usually to append a tactful paraphrase. We must gather that, although his audience is pleased to be showered with names like Clodius, Strabo, Eusebius, and Pomponius Mela, it is not at all an audience like the one Swift, say, was assuming. The world of Brydone and of his audience is far advanced in Whiggery (see, e.g., ɪɪ 285–286), skepticism, and scientism, although in aesthetics its tastes are still largely those of the Tories of the earlier part of the century.

III

Brydone is not merely attuned to register the ideas and attitudes most stylish in his day; he also is skilled in contriving the literary patterns of emotion most in vogue. As an example we can isolate from the literature of the second half of the century a pervasive ironic pattern of literary action, which we can term the pattern of comic reversal. Whether we meet it in fiction — and the works of Fielding and Smollett are full of it — in memoirs, in essays, or in travel books, the pattern is the same. It consists of two elements: we have first a protracted but smooth ascent to some height of optimistic illu-

Sicily in 1778. *Carte de la Sicile Moderne faite d'après de Nouvelles Observations en 1778.*
Map Division

sion; this condition is followed by a sudden reversal, a collapse into comic disillusion. One implication of the motif is that, although man's capacities for self-delusion are infinitely varied, it is yet possible for him partly to redeem himself from his labored fatuities by sudden, sometimes instinctual perceptions of his natural limitations. Another implication of the motif is its metaphorical significance as a rendering of the process of intellectual development, of the action of maturing: it is as if the eighteenth-century protagonist were condemned to re-enact constantly a sort of wry psychological, secular version of the action of losing a paradise.

Gulliver's experience with the Struldbrugs, in Chapter X of his Third Voyage, establishes the canonical form of the motif: after rhapsodizing for pages on the sublime possibilities for mankind in the prolongation of life, Gulliver is finally brought to enlightenment, whereupon he finds that his "keen appetite for perpetuity of life was much abated." The sense of shame usually accompanies the enlightenment portion of the total comic action, as if shame and humiliation — always associated with the loss of innocence — are inseparable concomitants of enlightenment. Moving forward to the 1760s, we find Boswell employing this motif of comic disillusion in the Louisa episode of his *London Journal.* His literary delight in shaping the naïve, illusioned narrative long after he has experienced its actual, disillusioning termination suggests that he had an acute eye and ear for the pattern of comic disillusion in much of the literature he admired. One work he admired greatly was *Rasselas,* whose structure can be said to constitute one great action of comic disillusion generated from the accumulation of many small analogous actions. We see the motif, for example, in Chapter VI, "A Dissertation on the Art of Flying," where ten paragraphs are devoted to the development of the Flying-Machine Projector's theories of flight, and where only one final paragraph is required to release both the projector and the listening Rasselas into enlightenment: ". . . he waved his pinions a while to gather air, then leaped from his stand, and in an instant dropped into the lake." The ten-to-one proportioning of the two elements of the ironic action here is common; illusions require days and weeks for their construction, but enlightenment takes but "an instant." The proportioning is similar in the following example, this one from Shenstone's *Essays on Men, Manners, and Things* (1764):

> Had I a fortune of 8 or 10,000 l. a year, I would methinks make myself a neighbourhood. I would first build a village with a church, and people it with inhabitants of some branch of trade that was suitable to the country round. I would then at proper distances erect a number of genteel boxes of about a 1000 l. a piece, and amuse myself with giving them all the advantages they could receive from taste. These would I people with a select number of well-chosen friends, assigning to each annually the sum of 200 l. for life. The salary should be irrevocable, in order to give them independency. The house, of a more precarious tenure, that, in cases of ingratitude, I might introduce another inhabitant.
>
> How plausible soever this may appear in speculation, perhaps a very natural and lively novel might be founded upon the inconvenient consequences of it, when put in execution.[16]

Turning now to Brydone, we can observe the skill and the sense of public gratification with which he manipulates this motif, and we can see the customary ethical intention in which the motif was most often enlisted. As Brydone and his friends depart from Naples by ship on a calm evening, we

---

[16] "Egotisms. From My Own Sensations."

are given six pages of rhapsodic description of the Bay of Naples, description which exploits the full resources of the standard imagery of the Sublime and the Beautiful. After luxuriating in "this delightful prospect," Brydone observes: "Our ship is going so smooth, that we are scarce sensible of the motion; and if this wind continue, before to-morrow night we shall be in sight of Sicily. Adieu. The captain is making a bowl of grog, and promising us a happy voyage." At this point Brydone has the reader entirely with him, and it is now time for the comic release. He proceeds: "16th [May, 1770]. All wrong — Sick to death — Execrable sirocc wind, and directly contrary — Vile heaving waves — A plague of all sea voyages" (i 25–26).

Again, while pausing on the top of Mt Etna, Brydone indulges in two pages of rapt speculation on the excellence of mountaintops as sites for philosophic meditation. Wrought to an elevation by the delightful prospect before both his outer and his inner eye, he is suddenly brought to earth — he sprains his ankle. He comments: "In the very midst of these meditations, my philosophy was at once overset, and in a moment I found myself relapsed into a poor miserable mortal; . . . and your poor philosopher was obliged to hop on one leg, with two men supporting him, for several miles over the snow" (i 218–219). We can hardly help recalling the findings of the speaker in Swift's *Mechanical Operation of the Spirit:* "Spiritual Intrigues . . . generally conclude like all others; they may branch upwards towards Heaven, but the Root is in the Earth. Too intense a Contemplation is not the Business of Flesh and Blood; it must by the necessary Course of Things, in a little Time, let go its Hold, and fall into *Matter*." The illustration employed by Swift to embody his point anticipates Brydone's ironic accident on Etna; Swift instances "that Philosopher, who, while his Thoughts and Eyes were fixed upon the *Constellations,* found himself seduced by his *lower Parts* into a *Ditch*."

Brydone's tendency to moralize overtly the action of comic disillusion is apparent also in another passage. On the boat trip from Catania to Syracuse, the travelers spy a large healthy turtle afloat in the water. Meditating on soup, they labor to maneuver the boat alongside. "He was already our own in idea, and we were only thinking of the various ways in which he should be dressed: — When — how vain and transitory all human possessions! the turtle made a plunge, slipped through [the boatmen's] fingers, and disappeared in a moment, and with him all our hopes. — We looked very foolish at each other, without uttering a word . . ." (i 286–287). It is clear that Brydone is not simply transcribing actual experience: what he is doing is locating pretexts for gratifying his audience's desire to see experience moralized by means of the pattern of comic reversal. The disappointments and embarrassments presented by Brydone sometimes take on the color of mock-heroic, indeed of mock-*Odyssey*. Leaving Malta by ship for Agrigento, he passes near the island of Gozzo, which he takes to be the ancient abode of Calypso. He writes: "You may believe we expected something very fine; but we were disappointed. . . . We looked, as we went along the coast, for the grotto of the goddess, but could see nothing that resembled it. Neither could we observe those verdant banks eternally covered with flowers; nor those lofty trees for ever in blossom, that lost their heads in the clouds, and afforded a shade to the sacred baths of her and her nymphs" (II 2–3). But here the absence of the "verdant banks eternally covered with flowers" mitigates the levity of the mock-naïve opening: we end with a tone which seriously recalls the Miltonic lost paradise. The mock-heroic ends, as it often does in eighteenth-century literature, in something close to real elegy.

Thus, unlike Hawkesworth's *Voyages*, which appealed through the sheer exoticism of Oceanic settings and customs quite soberly recorded, Brydone's *Tour* extended a more profound invitation to the reader of 1773. He must have encountered its received ideas and conventionalized emotional patterns with a delighted shock of recognition, for, as Johnson says of Gray's *Elegy*, it "abounds with images which find a mirror in every mind, and with sentiments to which every bosom returns an echo." And perhaps no image in the *Tour* made so powerful an appeal as the image of man which underlies these repeated patterns of comic reversal: despite his capacities for brisk locomotion, observation, and reportage, man is limited and frail, as his occasional awareness of some vague loss should remind him. It is this theme of the permanent limitations of man which allies writers so different as Swift and Burke, Johnson and Hume, and it is Brydone's expression of it which helps account for the popularity of his *Tour* and which gives him for us the appearance of a consummately representative man.[17]

---

[17] That the appeal of Brydone's *Tour* was not limited to England alone is indicated by the catalogue of the Lancaster (Massachusetts) Circulating Library, a collection of some fifty titles assembled in 1790–1791. As John D. Cushing points out, "The committee appointed to select the first titles obviously went about its work with great care" (*Bulletin of The New York Public Library* LXIV [August 1960] 433). The sixth accession, the catalogue indicates, was "Bridans tour thro' Scisily & Mal.ᵃ" Only after Brydone was safely laid in did the committee go on to acquire items like *The Spectator*, Lady Mary Wortley Montagu's *Letters*, Young's *Night Thoughts*, Thomson's *Seasons*, Gay's *Fables*, and *Paradise Lost*.

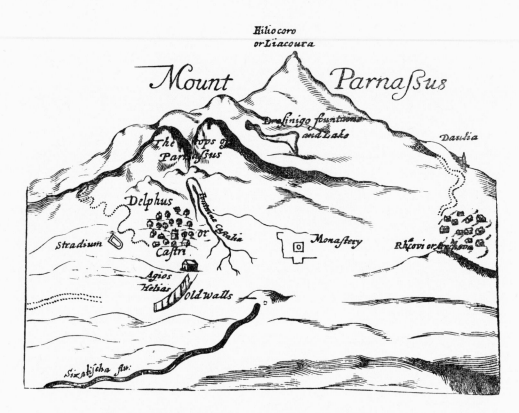

Map in Sir George Wheler's *A Journey into Greece* (1682 p 313).

Convention and Novelty in the Romantic Generation's Experience of Italy

By HERBERT BARROWS
University of Michigan

To live over people's lives is nothing unless we live over their perceptions, live over the growth, the change, the varying intensity of the same — since it was *by* these things they themselves lived.
— HENRY JAMES, *William Wetmore Story*

THE WORD in my title which I wish to emphasize is "experience." My point, and I shall try to illustrate it with reference to the Italian experience of Shelley and Byron, is that the study of the English literary traveler's interest in Italy ought to be focussed, more sharply than it has been in the past, on the exact nature and quality of each individual experience. Certainly the individual tour or sojourn has to be seen against the background of the experience of Italy that was generally available at the time. But it must also be seen in the context of the individual life, with its specific motivations and needs, and we should always try to study it in the light of a sympathetic awareness of what it means to be a traveler.

Foreign travel has been a possibility for the English private citizen since the very beginning of the eighteenth century, and the records of his travels — letters, diaries, and travel books as well as poems and novels — , even when we limit our attention to a single country such as Italy, constitute an almost overwhelming amount of material. Some of the most valuable studies of the English traveler's response to Italy have undertaken to reduce this mass of material to order by establishing a pattern of the growth, peak, and decline of the English enthusiasm for Italy and Italian values. A recent book, C. P. Brand's *Italy and the English Romantics*,[1] reaches a conclusion not very different from that reached by Roderick Marshall in the pioneer study of the subject, *Italy in English Literature 1755–1815*,[2] that the peak of the "Italianate fashion" came in the ten or twenty years immediately following the Napoleonic Wars, with the generation of Byron and Shelley, after which the pitch of enthusiasm suddenly declined. The standard here is the number of works of Italian literature published in England, the number of writers

---

[1] *Italy and the English Romantics: the Italianate Fashion in Early Ninteenth-Century England* (Cambridge 1957).
[2] *Italy in English Literature, 1755–1815: Origins of the English Romantic Interest in Italy* (New York 1934).

who made use of Italian forms or subject-matter, and the sheer volume of
enthusiasm with which spokesmen of this generation claimed to know and
love Italy.

Seen in the perspective afforded by such studies, there are three readily
distinguishable periods of English travel in Italy. First, there is the eighteenth
century as a whole, under the sign of the Grand Tour as a recognized insti-
tution. Second, there are the years from 1815 to 1830 when the Romantics
were coloring the experience of Italy with the legend of their lives and their
personalities. And third, there are the years from 1830 or 1840 right through
the end of the century and even into our own time (though this third period
is capable of further subdivision, especially in its latter stretches). In each
of these periods, the English traveler's experience of Italy had its characteristic modes and qualities, its characteristic features of content. And it might
be possible to place the peak in any one of the three, depending on the
criteria we use.

The eighteenth-century traveler, from Addison to Mrs Piozzi, was sometimes diffident about what he saw and sometimes downright grouchy. He
focussed on a narrow range of elements from the vast complex of elements
which later travelers have found in Italy, but he focussed on them with great
singleness of purpose. When we look back on the consistency with which
he pursued his vision of Italy — in a tour which lasted a year or two years
and was often extremely difficult — , we may wonder if he did not reach a
certain climax of functional perfection. At least he knew what he expected
from his tour, and most of his aims were realizable: later aims, beginning
with those of the Romantics, were not always to be so. The Romantic
experience was based to a much greater extent than is generally recognized
on the content of the eighteenth-century experience, to which it added a new
brand of enthusiasm, vehemence, and style: the Romantics certainly succeeded in dramatizing the idea of English devotion to Italy. Nevertheless,
for the kind of travel experience which is based on the sober, appreciative
knowledge of a very widely inclusive range of Italian values and achievements, we have to wait for the successive generations of Victorians.

It is a rare traveler who is able to move outside the limits of the pattern
of experience common to his time, but on the other hand it is only by close
scrutiny of the individual experience and not at all by statistics that we can
know what that pattern really was. The Romantic poets themselves — Byron
in the Fourth Canto of *Childe Harold*, for example — helped to create the
image according to which we see their generation as passionately enthusiastic
in its response to Italy, and the enthusiasm really did exist, really did give

a coloring, a direction to the works in which they wrote about Italy. But it is only an element, for any one of these travelers, in the totality of his day to day experience of Italy. If we go behind the accepted image to examine the actual experience, in even one or two instances, we gain a valuable corrective to some of our notions as to the exact place occupied by the Romantic generation in the development of this important cultural relationship.

The Italian experience of Shelley and Byron has been the subject of many special studies; and of course it has figured prominently in the general biographical and critical treatments of each poet and in the panoramic studies of the English in Italy. While there has not been unanimity as to just what Italy meant to each of them, the abiding impression, always invoked when a biographer or critic wishes to make a point on the basis of common assumptions, is that in their attitudes towards Italy, in the personal and literary values they derived from their Italian experience, the pattern of English response to Italy was at last fully realized.

And yet when this experience is scrutinized, it wears a certain equivocal air. It is neither so entirely new, so positive, or so completely and happily absorbed in Italian values as it has often been thought to be. All of which is, in many important respects, nothing against it. The critic can make himself ridiculous by seeming to prescribe, with such personalities as Shelley and Byron, what their experience *should* have been, what it might have been if they had been wiser, or better informed, or interested in this rather than that, or perhaps just more docile and ordinary.

But if it is foolish to prescribe after the fact, it is not foolish to wish to keep the record straight. To tell the story of the Italian experience of either of the two poets in full detail, and with adequate reference to the points on which there is agreement or disagreement among previous investigators, is not possible here, where our purpose is illustrative. In outline, however, their two stories are somewhat as follows.

With Shelley, the full story would begin with an attempt to distinguish the real motives that prompted him to leave England for Italy in the early spring of 1818, from the various declared motives. As early as the previous summer his letters begin to detail the symptoms of bad health which, as he no doubt believed and as he was especially anxious to convince Godwin, made it imperative to leave England for a warmer climate; finally he is declaring, "It is not health, but life, that I should seek in Italy." [3] The word "life" here

[3] *The Letters of Percy Bysshe Shelley*, ed Roger Ingpen (London 1909) II 565. Further references will be cited, immediately after the quotation, as *Letters*.

bears a double sense, which it would not have borne for earlier travelers, and the fuller sense involves a psychological urgency which produced the physical symptoms. It is reasonably clear that while Shelley himself believed that he had gone to Italy solely because his health forced him to do so, the particular symptoms of ill health which he noted in crescendo during these months were the results of his unconscious attempt to find a reason for leaving England which would be acceptable not only to Godwin but to himself. Among the real reasons for going were the pleasurable excitement he always found in travel and the delight with which he looked forward to seeing Italy. But a more important one was his anxiety to escape from the persecution and oppression which had gradually become inescapable in England. None of these reasons could be admitted either to himself or to others; and his health was instinctively enlisted as an excuse for the journey. (It is significant that in a letter to Keats urging him to come to Italy he said: "You ought, at all events, to see Italy, and your health which I suggest as a motive, may be an excuse for you." *Letters* II 809) In the first letter to Peacock from Italy, Shelley gives a more realistic explanation of the sense in which Italy meant the difference between life and death to him:

> . . . No sooner had we arrived at Italy, than the loveliness of the earth and the serenity of the sky made the greatest difference in my sensations. I depend on these things for life; for in the smoke of cities, and the tumult of human kind, and the chilling fogs and rain of our own country, I can hardly be said to live. (*Letters* II 591)

Shelley was not typical of his generation, or of later generations, but the fact is that with him, as with Byron, we see the beginning of a pattern of connections between the Italian journey on the one hand and very complex life-motives on the other which had not existed for the eighteenth-century traveler. The Grand Tourist, going over an itinerary that was prescribed in all its details, expected to receive a measureable accretion of knowledge from his visits to the best-known sites, monuments, and works of art, from his observation of men and manners. This knowledge he took back to England with him and applied it to the life in which the Grand Tour had been only an interlude. With Byron and Shelley, though they are not to be seen as sole instigators of the phenomenon, travel has become something more than a means for adding certain elements to an existing life-pattern. It has become a means for transforming the previous life, for remedying anything that was amiss with it (and not only economically or in terms of health), for challenging the old life. Given the right conditions in the traveler's relations to his own country, there is produced something that might be termed the "exile's complex"; and both Byron and Shelley were, as it happens, exiles. The words "life" and "live" in Shelley's letter to Peacock are symbolic of the expanded or heightened aims with which the Romantic generation began to undertake the sojourn in Italy.

With the other sentence from the same letter, about the loveliness of the earth and the serenity of the sky, we have an indication of what was to be the most important single element in Shelley's Italian experience. It was in the nature of his perceptive and imaginative processes to subject the world to an analysis which reduced it, in his experience, to its elements of earth, air, and water. The letters from Italy abound in evocations of "the green earth," in descriptions of the atmosphere, capable, for all its tenuous shifting and changing, of being fixed in exact notation; in descriptions of water, as the source of endless pleasures of sight and touch and motion. In his brief description of "the first things we met in Italy" —

> a ruined arch of magnificent proportions in the Greek taste, standing in a kind of road of green lawn, overgrown with violets and primroses, and in the midst of stupendous mountains, and a *blonde* woman of light and graceful manners, something in the style of Fuseli's Eve (*Letters* II 592) —

both woman and monumental arch are accessories which serve to point up the beauty of the landscape, a landscape which seems a fitter setting for a myth than for the incidents of real life. At its most positive, at the times when it reached its highest level of exhilaration, Shelley's response to Italy was a response to its natural elements, especially when they were seen as the surroundings for images and vestiges of the life of ancient Rome and, better still, of Greece

One of the most powerful imaginative responses that Shelley made during his years in Italy was that called forth at Pompeii by the beauty of its site and surroundings. As he and his companions sat under the colonnade of the temple of Jupiter he was moved to a vision of what life had been, in such places as this, for the Greeks who had inhabited them: for

> they lived in harmony with nature; and the interstices of their incomparable columns were portals, as it were, to admit the spirit of beauty which animates this glorious universe to visit those whom it inspired. If such is Pompeii, what was Athens? What scene was exhibited from the Acropolis, the Parthenon, and the temples of Hercules, and Theseus, and the Winds. The islands and the Aegean sea, the mountains of Argolis,

and the peaks of Pindus and Olympus, and the darkness of the Boeotian
forests interspersed. (*Letters* II 665)

At such moments Shelley's experience of Italy reached its greatest intensity:
and at such moments, it is easy to see, his experience was composed of two
elements: first, the Shelleyan response to the beauty of nature; and second,
his response to the stimulus afforded by the remains of classical antiquity.
For Shelley, Italy sometimes seems to have been a substitute for Greece.

In the areas of specifically Italian life and achievement, Shelley's responses
were either negative or conventional or both. The contemplation of man and
society in Italy afforded him no pleasure at all. His total impression, by July
25, was that "the modern Italians seem a miserable people, without sensi-
bility, or imagination, or understanding." Although this impression referred
to members of the upper classes whom he had met at the Casino at Bagni di
Lucca, a letter he wrote to Peacock from Ferrara on November 6, although
it contains a minute description of the farms he had seen on the journey from
Este, shows that he had been unable to make a sympathetic penetration of
the lives of the peasants he talked to. The few Italians who became members
of the Shelleys' circle of friends at Pisa a few years later were regarded as
exceptions to the rule that all Italians were uninteresting and unsympathetic,
until further acquaintance revealed that they, too, had, their weaknesses.
"There are *two* Italies," he declared in a letter to Leigh Hunt in December
1818 —

> one composed of the green earth and transparent sea, and the mighty
> ruins of ancient time, and aërial mountains, and the warm and radiant
> atmosphere which is interfused through all things. The other consists of
> the Italians of the present day, their works and ways. The one is the most
> sublime and lovely contemplation that can be conceived by the imagin-
> ation of man; the other is the most degraded, disgusting and odious.
> (*Letters* II 649)

Nothing in Shelley's later letters suggests that he ever revised the judgment
which he here expresses on the basis of nine or ten months' travel in Italy.
This failure to find anything commendable or interesting in the Italian people,
while we encounter it regularly in the eighteenth century, had already begun
by the time Shelley was in Italy to give way to more receptive attitudes.

One broad aspect of the national life did, however, make a strong impression on him. He saw the lower orders as a race of slaves whose lives presented
symbols of oppression and despair more lurid than any he had seen in England or Ireland. In Rome for the second time in the spring of 1819, after the

journey to Naples, he was shocked by seeing a band of fettered criminals, about three hundred in number, at work in the Square of St Peter's.

> The iron discord of those innumerable chains clanks up into the sonorous air, and produces, contrasted with the musical dashing of the fountains, and the deep azure beauty of the sky, and the magnificence of the architecture around, a conflict of sensations allied to madness. It is the emblem of Italy — moral degradation contrasted with the glory of the arts. (*Letters* II 687)

As for the glory of the arts, Shelley was pretty well content to follow the lead of his predecessors, certainly in the objects he chose to look at and often even in his responses to them. In the long letters to Peacock describing what he had seen in Rome we meet the same descriptions of the Forum and the Colosseum that we can find in the letters of almost any eighteenth-century traveler. Like his predecessors, he is far more interested in Roman than in post-Roman achievement; and like them, too, he was seeing according to a convention which set very narrow limits on what he was able to see. After describing his disappointment in St Peter's — "internally it exhibits littleness on a large scale, and is in every respect opposed to antique taste" — he is led back, by force of contrast, to the Pantheon. He then returns to modern times to describe the fountains of the Piazza Navona and the Piazza di Trevi; of the latter he says:

> The whole is not ill conceived nor executed; but you know not how delicate the imagination becomes by dieting with antiquity day after day! The only things that sustain the comparison are Raffael, Guido, and Salvator Rosa. (*Letters* II 682)

Shelley was a free spirit, if ever there was one, but these are not free judgments. (And far from rousing in us any sentiments of superiority, they may well remind us of the likelihood that our own personal tastes and judgments have been largely created by the judgments of our time.) The rigid exclusion of all post-classical achievement, only to allow Salvator Rosa to march in as one of three possible modern claims to glory, is evidence of the automatic acceptance of a convention that was well over a hundred years old and all but doomed in Shelley's own day. A good deal has been written about Shelley's response to the visual arts; but while a close study of the subject can be rewarding for what it tells us about Shelley, it offers us very little that we can regard as negotiable, or even interestingly suggestive, as accounts of the works themselves. The painters he mentions are Raphael,

Guido Reni, Correggio, Salvator Rosa, Guercino, Domenichino, the Caracci, Albani, Franceschini, Elisabetta Sirani, Titian, Michelangelo, and (in the belief that the Medusa in the Uffizi was his work) Leonardo. All of Michelangelo's chief virtues, as Sir Herbert Read has pointed out, struck him as defects; and any pictures painted before the fifteenth century — probably even before the sixteenth — he would have lumped together under some such heading as one guide-book reserved for them: "curious old pictures."

Tastes change, and once again we look with interest and admiration at the Carracci, at Guido Reni and Guercino, at Domenichino and Sassoferrato.

Guido Reni (1576–1642). The Infant Christ with St John.
Etching (Bartsch 13), The University of Michigan Museum of Art

Even so, it is a good deal less interesting than one might have hoped to look at pictures in Bologna with Shelley's descriptions of them in hand. His response to pictures is always literary; he does not view them as the result of specific choices of form and technique, but rather as absolute achievements, capable of being interpreted as directly as life itself. Of Raphael's St Cecilia he says, "You forget that it is a picture as you look at it" (*Letters* II 640). But that is not an unusual experience for him, since the saint's or madonna's smile was always the object of the same sort of attempt to penetrate its meaning, with its implications of a past and a future, as would appropriately be directed to the reading of a smile on a living countenance.

Shelley himself made no claims to connoisseurship in painting, and there is little evidence that his interest in Italian painting was not perfunctory as

well as conventional. What drew him to the galleries in Rome and Florence was the works of classical sculpture they contained. Reaching Florence in the autumn of 1819, he announced his purpose of "studying the gallery piecemeal," one of his chief objects in Italy being, as he said, "the observing in statuary and painting the degree in which, and the rules according to which, that ideal beauty, of which we have so intense yet so obscure an apprehension, is realized in external forms" (*Letters* II 726–727). But the notes he made there, as in Rome, dealt entirely with sculpture. His experience of sculpture seems to have been more intense than his experience of painting, and its importance in the development of his mind and art has received careful attention. That importance, it seems to me, is primarily

Marc Antonio Raimondi (born c 1488). St Cecilia, after Raphael. *Engraving, Prints Division*

a philosophical one. He viewed the works of sculpture he saw in Italy, whether Greek or Roman, as a means for achieving an understanding of the Greek approach to the problem of expressing ideal beauty. In fact, he approached painting and sculpture at the point at which, the technical part of the artist's work having been done, they resembled rather than differed from one another. At this point they also resembled poetry, at least for

Shelley, so that the poet could turn to them for lessons which could be directly applied to his task of rendering ideal truth and beauty in humanly apprenhensible forms.

All this constitutes an aesthetic, to be sure, and that for Shelley it was a valid aesthetic is demonstrated by his success in transmuting motifs from his experience of the arts into the characteristically rarefied element of his poetry, where they indeed play their occasionally traceable part in the creation of "beautiful idealisms of moral excellence." But it should be noted that at the beginning of this process which ended in such splendid metamorphosis, there was an experience of works of art which relied entirely on convention and which, whatever its validity and richness for Shelley, does nothing to enhance our sense of the presence or significance either of the works he mentions or of art in general.

Back in Florence in 1821 (*Letters* II 885), he writes to Mary at Pisa,

> I spent three hours this morning principally in the contemplation of the Niobe, and of a favorite Apollo; all worldly thoughts and cares seem to vanish from before the sublime emotions such spectacles create; and I am deeply impressed with the great difference of happiness enjoyed by those who live at a distance from these incarnations of all that the finest minds have conceived of beauty, and those who can resort to their company at pleasure.

I do not suggest that the delight in contemplation was not genuine, or that the Niobe and the favorite Apollo were not worthy of being contemplated with delight, but merely that we see here an instance of the traveler abandoning himself uncritically to values guaranteed by the received opinion of his time, so that the response is very highly subjective. It is Shelley's idealizing power which gave value to this experience, and unless we possess the same power there is nothing in it for us to emulate. This, it seems to me, is the typical distribution of values in Shelley's experience of Italy. At such times as he was happy there, the light and air, the ancient monuments, certain works of art, produced a lifting of the spirit which carried him into the realm of his most fruitful contemplation and creativity. In a sense, the influence behind all this was Italy, but Shelley's experience of more specifically Italian values, Italian achievement, was restricted enough, even commonplace. What he made of it — and not only in the sense of something that he put into his poetry, but in the sense of the élan of the day-to-day experience itself, when it was at its best — we should certainly call distinguished and are kept from doing so only by the thought that we probably ought to call it sublime.

He was certainly not always happy in Italy, and in the darker side of his years there we recognize an element that will occasionally figure in the post-Romantic experience of Italy, as a potential if not inevitable concomitant of the traveler's desire to make a complete substitution of the new life for the old. Expatriates there had been even in the eighteenth century, for reasons of health or economy, and we need not point out how often in Victorian biography we encounter the pattern of a prolonged domesticity in Italy. Shelley and Byron, however, were not expatriates but exiles. Writing to Thomas Medwin in January 1820, and urging him to come to Italy for its climate and its art, Shelley calls Italy "the Paradise of exiles, the retreat of pariahs." "But," he adds, "I am thinking of myself rather than of you."

The circumstances under which both poets had left England were, to say the least, special; and there were actual legal obstacles to their returning which make it not strictly necessary to look for metaphysical ones. Granted these harsh facts, however, we see in the two poets' varied and characteristic reactions to their expatriation an illustration of attitudes that occur fairly frequently in the annals and the experience of the post-Romantic traveler, down to and including our own time.

It all begins when we see the word "life" figuring in a writer's proclamation of his travel aims, when the idea starts to take shape that essential rewards can be obtained by going to the new country to live, or at any rate to settle down for a prolonged stay. A new ideal comes in, with its virtues and its values no doubt, but also with its own vices and its own possibilities for foolishness: the ideal of entering the life of the new country from the inside, of penetrating it with complete sympathy and knowledge. It should be noted that even while he entertains this ideal the traveler remains English or American in certain important respects, for he usually has no intention of taking up work or citizenship in the country in question. Right here there enters the possibility of a confusion of aim, the possibility that the traveler is making demands of himself and his experience that he will ultimately be unable to fulfill. Perhaps the hidden principle that underlies these claims may be seen as the traveler's willingness to give absolute, rather than contingent, value to the exotic.

When the traveler has undergone some deeply painful experience in his own country, when it has rejected him or failed to treat him as he thinks he should be treated, then there may come into being the emotional pattern of opposing tensions which we have already described as the exile's complex. Under less crucial circumstances, the new post-Romantic ideal results in the pursuit of a mystique which, while it has certainly thickened and intensified

and subtilized the traveler's potential experience, has also added many a
spiritual burden to his lot. Attendant on this mystique is a host of typically
modern snobbisms: the cult of the undiscovered, the pursuit of the truly
native and characteristic, the dread (in James's phrase) of "the foot-fall of
the detested fellow-pilgrim." Attendant on it also is a certain amount of
inevitable disappointment, and the likelihood that when things go wrong
the eager, uncritical enthusiasm will turn to bitterness and contempt.

Not all of this is the fault of Shelley and Byron, to be sure, but they do
afford early, premonitory instances of what may happen to the modern
traveler who is prompted to substitute *life* in the new country for life in
the old, to set one up in opposition to the other. Shelley in particular, with
his aristocrat's aloofness and his eclecticism, can scarcely be said to have
sought too deep a penetration of life around him in Italy. But intermingled
with the many passages in his letters which describe the delights of the new
life, his satisfaction with the bargain, there are also many, beginning early
and recurring up to the end, which describe a homesickness whose bitterness
was compounded by the sense that he had willingly rejected what he now
missed.

> All that I see in Italy — and from my tower window I now see the mag-
> nificent peaks of the Apennines half enclosing the plain — is nothing;
> it dwindles into smoke in the mind, when I think of some familiar forms
> of scenery, little perhaps in themselves, over which old remembrances
> have thrown a delightful colour. How we prize what we despised when
> present! So the ghosts of our dead associations rise and haunt us, in
> revenge for our having let them starve, and abandoned them to perish.
> (*Letters* ɪɪ 709)

These are the realities of Shelley's Italian experience, too, just as much as "the
Praxitelean shapes that throng the Vatican, the Capitol, and the palaces of
Rome," or the happiness of the last summer at Lerici — "this divine bay" —
reading Calderon, sailing, listening to "the most enchanting music," regretting only that "the summer must ever pass." To ignore them, or to ignore
the comparative narrowness of it all, is to give an account of Shelley's Italian
experience that is both naive and false and that will sooner or later break
down when it is pressed into service for critical or biographical purposes.

Byron's sojourn in Italy was longer than Shelley's and the records of it,
in the *Letters and Journals* [4] as well as in contemporary memoirs, are full

---

[4] *The Works of Lord Byron: Letters and Journals*, ed R. E. Prothero, 6 vols (London 1922–24).
References will be cited, immediately after the quotation, as *Letters and Journals*.

and detailed. Like Shelley's, Byron's Italian experience was in many areas the conventional experience of his time and, hence, of the preceding century; like Shelley, Byron made on the basis of such experiences something new and highly personal that transposed the English traveler's potential response into a new and higher key. The fourth canto of *Childe Harold* was at once the apotheosis and the swan-song of the Grand Tour. A reader accustomed to jogging up and down the peninsula with the eighteenth-century tourist will always know what is coming next in this poem, and yet everything is new, not merely altered by being used as a backdrop for the dramatic figure of Byron himself, but transfigured by style and energy of treatment. The poem's basis in first-hand experience was the rudimentary and fairly blasé version of the Grand Tour in which Byron was engaged off and on from the fall of 1816 to the spring of 1817, helped out by Hobhouse's notes and by Byron's reading in such works as Dr John Moore's *Italy* [5] and Mrs Hemans' *Restoration of the Works of Art to Italy*.[6] Considered from the point of view of the materials that went into it, of what it was in any objective sense about, the poem is a *tour de force* in which Byron succeeds in giving a remarkably new kind of life to an old experience about which he was sometimes cynical — "all that time-tax of travel," in the phrase he used for the sights of Verona — but which at most times he saw from an entirely traditional point of view. Nothing needs to be said about the role played by Byron's familiarity with Italian literature (whatever the debt to Whistlecraft in the entire transaction) in creating the form and spirit of *Don Juan*. It is customary to point out that in *Beppo*, based as it was on Byron's familiarity with Venetian domestic life, Byron widened the ranged and altered the tone of Italian subject matter that was available for treatment by English writers. Here too, in a way, something new was being made from something old. The figure of the cicisbeo had fascinated the eighteenth-century commentators, but they never felt that they knew the whole story of his functions: perhaps Byron was a little late, but he felt that at last he had the answers to their questions.

These and other aspects of Byron's demonstrable literary debt to Italy have been explored in detail, though often with too naive an approach to the questions of what constitutes indebtedness and of the way a writer's personal experience enters the fabric of his work. At the moment, however, if the record is to be kept accurate it ought to be corrected by an analytic reading of the personal side of Byron's Italian experience. C. P. Brand, in the work

[5] *A View of the Society and Manners in Italy: with Anecdotes relating to some Eminent Characters.* 2 vols (London 1781).
[6] London 1816.

mentioned earlier (p 12), pointing out that there were English travelers who remained aloof from Italian life and others who entered into it closely, cites Byron as being among the few Englishmen who, in his own words, had lived "in their houses and in the heart of their families . . . long enough . . . to feel more for them as a nation than for any other in existence." Comparatively speaking, Byron's claim was just, but if we come to it after having traced his experience and his attitudes as they shifted and developed during his years in Italy, it will be seen to mean both more and less than it means when we encounter it out of context.

Byron's attitudes towards Italy — among them the affection which he often proclaimed and no doubt sincerely felt, the desire to think of himself as having been completely assimilated into Italian life, as well as the negative attitudes, the contempt and disgust which sometimes assailed him — must all be seen primarily as functions of his attitude towards England. He was there in the first place because life had become impossible in England, and the psychological mechanism by which he set Italy, the richness and exclusiveness of his Italian experience, up against the country which had rejected him, is perfectly obvious. For example in 1819, in a letter to Murray, he says,

> Besides, I mean to write my best work in *Italian*, and it will take me nine years more thoroughly to master the language; and then if my fancy exist, and I exist too, I will try what I *can* do *really*. As to the Estimation of the English which you talk of, let them calculate what it is worth, before they insult me with their insolent condescension. (*Letters and Journals* IV 284–285)

Italy, and his Italian interests, offered him the possibility of feeling, and of announcing as fact whenever it seemed necessary, that he had loftily withdrawn himself from further competition for glory in English letters. Meanwhile, the life he was leading in Italy must be made to seem, at least, to exceed in charm and ease, in freedom from stupid constraint, the life he might have led in England.

Often it did seem to do so, and no doubt his years in Italy offered him as much happiness as he could have found anywhere. But at other times the happiness must have seemed to him, as it seems to us, to be built up from frail, pinchbeck materials. The Venetian family life into which he had gained an entrée gradually came to seem not only corrupt but endlessly boring. Later, for about a year beginning in the spring of 1820, the activities of the insurgents around Ravenna promised excitement and a chance for serious action; but the insurrection refused to come to a boil. At such times, when the charm or interest failed, all Byron saw about him was a country that was not his own. He could pretend, as he does for example in a letter to Francis Hodgson, written from Ravenna in December 1820, to have become almost more Italian than English:

> . . . What I have been doing would but little interest you, as it regards another country and another people, and would be almost speaking another language, for my own is not quite so familiar to me as it used to be. (*Letters and Journals* v 140)

But ten days later, he is recording in his journal his disappointment at receiving no letters from England: "Very sulky in consequence (for there ought to have been letters), and ate in consequence a copious dinner; for which I am vexed, it makes me swallow quicker — but drank very little" (v 147). He could be as vehement as any traveler has ever been in his distaste for the figure cut by his compatriots abroad — "a parcel of staring boobies, who go about gaping and wish to be at once cheap and magnificent" (iv 79–80), but Trelawny, speaking of Byron's prolonged absence from England, said that "it had not effaced the mark John Bull brands his children with; the instant he loomed above the horizon, on foot or horseback, you saw at a glance he was a Britisher." And Trelawny (not always a trustworthy witness, to be sure) adds, "He did not understand foreigners, nor they him; and, during the time I knew him, he associated with no Italians except the family of Count Gamba." [7]

I hope it is clear that I am not trying to reduce Byron's experience, ultimately, to the commonplace. Again I would merely suggest, as with Shelley, that his Italian experience is not the uniformly positive, glowing, happy affair that it has sometimes thoughtlessly been described as being, and that we should not take Byron's own assessment of it, at his most enthusiastic or most wistful moments, as the whole story. Distinction there certainly is, and a truly creative originality, but these qualities can be rightly appraised only if we see them as they emerge from a total experience which was not exempt from the laws, and the all too human impulses, which operate whenever it is a question of the travel experience.

One cannot have been in Italy very long before becoming aware, if only from the commemorative plaques on palace walls, that one has had remarkable predecessors, writers especially, who might be expected to have interesting things to say about all that one is seeing. Gradually, with the requisite humility, one develops the habit of comparing their responses with

7 Edward John Trelawny, *Records of Byron, Shelley, and the Author* (New York) 1887) 26.

one's own — and although it is true that some see better than others, that less has been lost on some individual travelers than on others, on some generations than on others, still all the responses are interesting, so long as they are genuine, all have something to add to our understanding of the most inexhaustibly interesting of countries. But if what they saw helps us, if the very *way* they saw often gives us a capacity of vision which we could not have attained without them, it might also be remembered that when we undertake to study their responses, to analyze them and make comparisons among them, something will be gained if we bring to bear on our study anything we may have learned at first hand about the traveler's lot: if in reading travel literature we will try not to forget what it is to be a traveler.

"Dr. Syntax tumbling into the Water," from William Combe, *The Tour of Doctor Syntax in Search of the Picturesque* (London [1812] 1865) facing p 87.

*   *   *

An heap of stones the Doctor found,
Which loosely lay upon the ground,
To form a seat, where he might trace
The antique beauty of the place:

But, while his eye observed the line
That was to limit the design,
The stones gave way, and sad to tell,
Down from the bank he headlong fell.   (p 87)

The Road to Reality:

Burlesque Travel Literature and
Mark Twain's *Roughing It*

By Franklin R. Rogers
The University of California, Davis

IN JULY, 1870, Elisha Bliss of the American Publishing Company completed a contract with Samuel L. Clemens, the latest arrival among the ranks of the American comic writers, which called for the delivery by January 1 1871 of sufficient manuscript to make a 600-page book. Bliss, of course, expected the author to furnish something which would repeat the success of *The Innocents Abroad*, which had been published the previous year, and Clemens proposed to outdo himself, if possible, this time with a tale based upon his trip across the Plains in 1861 and his six years' sojourn in Nevada and California. The six months allotted by the contract proved entirely too short for the completion of the projected book. The protracted illness and finally the death of Clemens' father-in-law, Jervis Langdon, and the illness and death of a house-guest, Emma Nye, consumed much of the author's time, and progress on the manuscript was further retarded by a dissatisfaction with the product of his labors which led to extensive revisions. Even an additional six months did not free him from the sense of pressure. As a result, the book which he finally produced exhibits at least two major flaws. One is the awkward break in tone, structure, and point of view evident in the last eighteen chapters, the consequence of his hasty incorporation at the last moment of the series of letters written from Hawaii for the Sacramento *Union* in 1866. The other is the padding of the text with statistics and quotations, principally from his newspaper clippings, which characterizes a number of the earlier chapters. But despite its imperfections the book proved quite acceptable to Bliss, and its subsequent success apparently stilled any misgivings Twain himself may have had on the score of his patchwork. Interested as he no doubt was in securing another comic best-seller, Bliss ignored its faults; he probably also failed to appreciate the essential importance of the manuscript which Clemens sent him in batches during the first months of 1871. For while *Roughing It* marks the culmination of a seventy-year-old tradition in burlesque travel literature, it also represents the successful transformation of burlesque travel literature conventions into the means for significant literary expression.

The tradition to which *Roughing It* owes a substantial debt begins with William Combe's *The Tour of Dr. Syntax in Search of the Picturesque* which first appeared serially in the *Poetical Magazine,* 1809–1811. Written in a pseudo-Hudibrastic verse which "may wel be rym dogerel," the tour proved a popular success. Combe exploited its popularity with an edition in book form in 1812 and two sequels, *The Second Tour of Dr. Syntax in Search of Consolation* (1820) and *The Third Tour of Dr. Syntax in Search of a Wife* (1821); during the next half-century several British publishers managed to keep the three tours before the reading public.[1] As the title of the first poem suggests, it is a burlesque of the popular late eighteenth-century literature of picturesque travel to which Wordsworth's *An Evening Walk* and *Descriptive Sketches* are closely related. In its general conception Combe's poem reflects the work of such writers of picturesque travel poetry as Anthony Champion, Thomas Maude, and George Cumberland; the central figure, Dr Syntax, is a caricature of William Gilpin, Rector of Boldre, who has been fittingly called "the high priest of the picturesque."[2] George Crabbe reacted to this literature with a grim realism which a hundred years later won Edwin Arlington Robinson's admiration; Combe reacted with a satire conveyed primarily through his character, Dr Syntax, whose excessive fastidiousness and sublimity of taste cause him to reject and suppress the disturbing truths which Crabbe fastened upon. Dr Syntax is the very quintessence of the artist in search of the picturesque, the artist who, in order to achieve the picturesque, must take liberties with the actuality before him, blinding himself to that which offends his taste and freely substituting from his imagination that which will heighten his gratification, thus forcing the observed reality into a preconceived ideal pattern of the picturesque. "What man of taste," Dr Syntax asks,

> my right will doubt,
> To put things in, or leave them out?
> 'Tis more than right, it is a duty,
> If we consider landscape beauty:
> He ne'er will as an artist shine,
> Who copies Nature line by line.[3]

According to Combe, this character stems from the mock-heroic tradition; in Canto XII of the first tour, he wrote:

---

[1] At least ten English editions and reprints appeared between 1821 and 1868.
[2] Christopher Hussey, *The Picturesque* (London and New York 1927) 111.
[3] *Doctor Syntax's Three Tours* (London 1868) 7.

> You'll see, at once, in this Divine,
> Quixote and Parson Adams shine:
> An hero well combin'd you'll view
> For FIELDING and CERVANTES too.   (p 41)

Certainly in structure, the Dr Syntax poems are a derivative of the knight-errant tradition on which *Don Quixote* is built, but, despite the doctor's encounter with highwaymen which is in the same vein as the battle with the huntsman's hounds in *Joseph Andrews*, very little of the mock-heroic actually appears in the series. An important difference between Don Quixote and Dr Syntax is that Cervantes' character is deranged, totally dissociated from the actuality through which he moves; the doctor perceives the actuality, but for reasons of taste ignores some aspects of it and, ignorant of worldly matters, fails to understand others. Instead, in his extreme sentimentality and his frequent soliloquies upon picturesque or melancholy scenes, he is much closer to Mr Yorick of Sterne's *Sentimental Journey.*

The popularity of Dr Syntax and his adventures is demonstrated not only by the frequent editions and reprints but also by the extent to which subsequent humorists resorted to them for guidance in shaping their own burlesques of travel literature. Apparently it was not so much the doctor's pretense to refined taste and sentiment which attracted the later humorists as it was the comic possibilities inherent in the coupling of this attitude with his artistic and scientific aspirations. Armed with sketchbook and notebook, the doctor traveled about England ever ready to preserve the picturesque scene which fluttered his pulse or the "curious" information which excited his mind. As a result of this combination, a third dimension, as it were, could be added to the burlesque. Not only is the reader moved to laughter by the contrast between the traveler's expectations and the actuality encountered; he is also moved to laughter by the traveler's subsequent interpretations in the form of wretched poetry, crude drawings, or fantastic scientific theories. A host of similar travelers, each equipped with sketchbook or notebook or both and eager to present the results of his travels to the reading public, crowd the pages of the British comic magazines down through the first twenty years of *Punch*, that is, from the 1840s to the 1860s, and appear in such less well-known humor magazines as *Fun*, *Judy*, and *Punch and Judy*. But only two of Dr Syntax's progeny, Thackeray's Michael Angelo Titmarsh and Dickens' Mr Samuel Pickwick, P.C., have won a permanent place in literature.[4]

4 Franklin R. Rogers, *Mark Twain's Burlesque Patterns* (Dallas 1960) 30–35. Further information, especially on Combe's influence on *The Pickwick Papers*, appears in Wilhelm Dibelius, "Zu den *Pickwick Papers*," *Anglia* xxxv (1912) 101–110.

Imitative of the British periodicals, the American humor magazines also afford several examples of the type. Generally, the American humorists appear to have modelled their work after the current British burlesques, without any direct reference to the original tours of Dr Syntax, but in at least one instance the American by-passed the contemporary British examples and returned directly to Combe's work. In the first issue of his *Illustrated California Magazine* (1856), J. M. Hutchings began a burlesque entitled "Dr. Dotitdown in Search of the Picturesque, Arabesque, Grotesque, and Burlesque." The title contains, of course, references to Combe's *Tour of Dr. Syntax in Search of the Picturesque* and to Poe's *Tales of the Grotesque and Arabesque.*

By the 1860s Combe's conception had undergone several mutations. One was the very early abandonment of his doggerel verse in favor of prose; another was the addition of a traveling companion who bears a distant relationship to Sancho Panza, a more immediate one to Sam Weller. A vernacular character, this companion, usually a servant or a young relative or family friend, serves a function slightly different from Sancho Panza's. As far as the reader is concerned, one of Sancho's major services is to report the actuality which the Knight, because of his delusions, cannot see. The companion of the nineteenth-century burlesque constantly reminds the reader and the traveler himself of those unpicturesque elements of the actuality which the traveler has chosen to ignore, and contributes a knowledge, sometimes surprisingly full for one of his years, in those fields where the traveler, in his innocence, is totally uninitiated: the properties of a wide variety of strong beverages, the wiles of worldly women, the art of gambling, and the devices of a wide variety of tricksters, swindlers, and other petty criminals. With predilections for such activities as those indicated by his knowledge, the companion is the major source of conflict for the traveler. With the emergence of the companion, this type of burlesque, some fifty years after Dr Syntax first set out on his sway-backed mare, had become fairly conventional: the traveler is a refined and sophisticated gentleman bent upon studying art, discovering sources for other ponds of Hampstead, or devising further theories of tittlebats; his companion is his antithesis in taste, sentiments, and interests; their itinerary takes the pair to scientific wonders, monuments of antiquity, or paintings of the Masters; and a series of arguments and mishaps, precipitated by the companion, disappoint or deflate the gentleman's expectations.

The conventional character of these burlesques is suggested not only by the frequent reappearance of the same elements but also by the failure of the British magazines to keep pace with developments in travel literature. Long after the focus of interest in travel books had shifted from the haunts of the Romantics in Italy, France, and Germany, to scenes of intrepid adventure in the Near East, the Orient, Africa, and the western United States, the travelers in the burlesques still studied their art in the Louvre and the Capitol and sought the picturesque in the Lake District, the Rhine Valley, the Black Forest, and the Harz Mountains. The result, in the British magazines of the 1860s, was a dissociation of the burlesques from the literature upon which they should have fed, with a consequent loss of vitality which is reflected in the mutation of the central character, who is reduced from a caricature of the sentimental traveler to a simple straightman. No longer mad, not even north-north-west, he has become to a great degree merely the center from which we measure the antics of his ebullient companion and others. The mutation is quite visible in one of the longest of such burlesques, "Our Roving Correspondent," which began in the first issue of *Punch* for 1860. In the July 27 1861 issue, the refined traveler, Jack Easel, comments upon young female tourists at the Italian art galleries:

> The ease and rapidity with which these charming critics form acquaintance with and discuss the merits of the Old Masters is truly astonishing. I once heard a young lady . . . remark, that she had "done" the Capitol between the hours of breakfast and lunch, adding that she would be able to give me a full description of the Borghese Collection by the time we met at dinner. "*Per Bacco!* Ma'am," I exclaimed — you know we were in Italy, and I always ejaculate, if possible in the language of the country where I am residing — "*per Bacco!* What a muff is your humble servant. Here have I been spending months in the study of a single gallery and am half inclined to throw up my profession in despair, at my ignorance."

Although the comment about ejaculations suggests the exaggerated sophistication of earlier travelers who did things "by the book," the passage in general demands that the reader regard Jack Easel as the standard against which the charming critics are measured and found wanting.

In the United States the type retained a great deal of its vitality simply because, while British readers were exploring the mysteries of the Middle East in such books as Warburton's *The Crescent and the Cross*, Curzon's *Monasteries of the Levant*, and Burton's *A Pilgrimage to Al-Medinah and Meccah*, the Americans were re-discovering a picturesque Europe in such books as Sara Jane Lippincott's *Haps and Mishaps of a Tour in Europe*, Harriet Beecher Stowe's *Sunny Memories of Foreign Lands*, and Bayard Taylor's *Views A-Foot*. As Professor Willard Thorp has noted in his study of such American travel books:

> The less imaginative of the professional writers soon evolved a sort of standard pattern for the travel book. The author must begin with the

excitements of the ocean voyage itself and devote at least a portion of a chapter to the thrill, so long anticipated, of setting foot on foreign soil. From this point on he should mix architecture and scenery . . . , skillfully work in a little history . . . , taking care to add a touch of sentiment or eloquence when the occasion permitted. If the essay or book required a little padding, it was always possible to retell an old legend or slip in an account of dangers surmounted in crossing the Alps.[5]

That is, the travel books which American writers were producing lent themselves well to the sort of burlesque treatment we have been considering; it is not surprising to find them getting such treatment from Artemus Ward, Petroleum V. Nasby, J. Ross Browne, and, of course, Mark Twain.

In *The Innocents Abroad*, the most famous burlesque product of this spate of American travel books, we find Mark Twain building upon the pattern which Thorp has noted. The first paragraph contains a passage which is, with its alliterations, rhythms, hyperboles, and clichés, at once a revelation of the delusions of the passengers and a parody of the effusive statements of anticipatory thrills in the books upon which it is modelled:

> [The passengers] were to sail for months over the breezy Atlantic and the sunny Mediterranean; they were to scamper about the decks by day, filling the ship with shouts and laughter — or read novels and poetry in the shade of the smoke-stacks, or watch for the jelly-fish and the nautilus, over the side, and the shark, the whale, and other strange monsters of the deep; and at night they were to dance in the open air, on the upper deck, in the midst of a ballroom that stretched from horizon to horizon, and was domed by the bending heavens and lighted by no meaner lamps than the stars and the magnificent moon — dance, and promenade, and smoke, and sing, and make love, and search the skies for constellations that never associate with the "Big Dipper" they were so tired of: and they were to see the ships of twenty navies — the customs and costumes of twenty curious peoples — the great cities of half a world — they were to hobnob with nobility and hold friendly converse with kings and princes, Grand Moguls, and the anointed lords of mighty empires!

But although *The Innocents Abroad* is a burlesque of travel literature, the controlling fiction of the conventional Dr Syntax type of burlesque, the conflict between a sentimental traveler and his irrepressible companion, is missing, or rather is subordinated to such an extent that it appears only in occasional episodes.

The Innocents Abroad is actually an intermediate stage in a series of experiments through which Twain gradually shaped the burlesque conven-

---

[5] "Pilgrim's Return," *Literary History of the United States*, ed Robert E. Spiller, et al (New York 1953) 831.

tions to his own artistic purposes. The first stage in the sequence dates from 1866, when Twain built the controlling fiction of his Sandwich Islands letters directly upon the conventional traveler-companion conflict. Adopting for these letters the pose of Mr Twain, a traveler with all the sensibilities and most of the aspirations of Dr Syntax, and creating a companion, Mr Brown, as bitter an enemy to sentiment as any of his predecessors, Twain tried to

"Innocent Dreams," from Twain's *Roughing It* (1872) p 21.

fulfill the two major conditions of his contract with the Sacramento *Union*, that he write a humorous travel sketch and that he furnish factual information about the Hawaiian Islands for the *Union* readers. The attempt to fulfill these two conditions involved Twain directly in a problem inherent in this type of burlesque from its beginnings: how to convey to the reader a clear concept of the actuality which moves the sophisticated traveler to sentimental tears or his companion to snorts of derision. As long as the burlesque is written in the third person, there is no problem. The author, on his own authority, presents the actuality and then permits the two characters to give their interpretations of it. But when, as in the greater portion of the burlesques of this type, the author chooses the first person form of narration, the problem becomes central. Whether he adopts for himself the pose of the traveler or the companion, he must accept as the price a blindness to and ignorance of certain elements in the actuality before him. Of course, he may very easily work in the reactions and interpretations of his associate as, from his point of view, shocking examples of blindness or ignorance, but the reader must discern the actuality for himself somewhere between the two extremes resulting from the traveler's exaggerated sentimentality and the companion's exaggerated skepticism and unregeneracy.

Here we can perceive what may well have been the reason for the failure of the British burlesques to keep pace with the mid-century developments in travel literature. As long as the books being burlesqued dealt with countries which the anticipated audience knew with a fair degree of intimacy, the humorist could depend upon the reader's knowledge to supply the information which his chosen pose prevented him from presenting in the burlesque. But when British travelers pushed on into new and relatively unknown regions, the humorist could not follow unless he forged new tools for his art. Mark Twain faced exactly the same problem, but one cannot say he solved it; he merely ignored the demands of consistency, slipping easily out of his pose to the role of reporter as frequently as he wished, apparently without even asking himself whether such a course indicated Emersonian greatness or artistic weakness.

The letters written for the *Alta Californian* describing Twain's journey from San Francisco to New York by way of the Isthmus in 1866–67 and the *Quaker City* excursion retain the same controlling fiction and exhibit the same disregard for consistency, but in the reworking of these letters for *The Innocents Abroad* Twain took the first major step toward the achievement of *Roughing It* when he attempted to fuse the characteristics of the traveler and his companion in one narrator. The fusion involved him in further difficulties, for this new narrator must exhibit on the one hand the sophistication and sentimentality of the traveler, on the other the uncouthness and insensitivity of the companion, and as necessary the judiciousness of the reporter. Once again he ignored the demands of consistency and let the contradictions stand. For example, his narrator is disdainful of sentimental tears after weeping over the graves of Abelard and Heloise and then learning their history, but he weeps as copiously as either Dr Syntax or Mr Yorick when he views Adam's tomb. Then, in order to justify his denunciation of William C. Prime's sentimental tears on the shores of Galilee, Twain must cast his narrator in the role of a clear-eyed and judicious reporter of the observed reality.

In that portion of *Roughing It* which concludes with the departure for the Sandwich Islands, Twain devised a method of reconciling the opposed points of view. *Roughing It* opens with a passage which is both similar to and subtly and significantly different from the statement of anticipatory thrills in the first pages of *The Innocents Abroad*:

I was young and ignorant, and I envied my brother. I coveted his distinction and his financial splendor, but particularly and especially the long, strange journey he was going to make, and the curious new world he was going to explore. He was going to travel! I never had been away from home, and that word "travel" had a seductive charm for me. Pretty soon he would be hundreds and hundreds of miles away on the great plains and deserts, and among the mountains of the Far West, and would see buffaloes and Indians, and prairie dogs, and antelopes, and have all kinds of adventures, and maybe get hanged or scalped, and have ever such a fine time, and write home and tell us all about it, and be a hero. And he would see the gold mines and the silver mines, and maybe go about of an afternoon when his work was done, and pick up two or three pailfuls of shining slugs, and nuggets of gold and silver on the hillside. And by and by he would become very rich, and return home by sea, and be able to talk as calmly about San Francisco and the ocean, and "the isthmus" as if it was nothing of any consequence to have seen those marvels face to face.

The significant difference is in the pronoun used in each instance. The pronoun *they* in the earlier passage directs the ridicule toward the other *Quaker City* passengers and to travelers who write travel books. It implicitly exempts the narrator himself. The shift in point of view to the first person in the *Roughing It* passage focuses the ridicule upon the narrator himself and tends to remove travelers as a class to the background, if not out of the picture.

A change of plan during the composition of *Roughing It* reveals Twain's struggle with the problem of the point of view. On March 4 1871 he wrote to his brother, Orion, that "right in the first chapter I have got to alter the whole style of one of my characters and re-write him clear through to where I am now."[6] Since the narrator himself is the only character who appears with sufficient frequency to require the sort of extensive revision suggested by this comment, the letter reflects some important discovery Twain had made relative to the point of view to be used, and his determination to act upon it.[7] The discovery was made as Twain pored over several letters he had written to the Keokuk *Gate City* in 1861 and '62 describing his adventures in Nevada, and therefore was apparently connected with them.[8] In these letters, Twain had adopted the pose of an unsophisticated, unregenerate "bitter enemy to sentiment" whose letters home were designed primarily to

[6] *Mark Twain's Letters*, ed A. B. Paine (New York and London 1917) i 186.
[7] On this question see also Henry Nash Smith, "Mark Twain as an Interpreter of the Far West: The Structure of *Roughing It*," *The Frontier in Perspective*, ed Walker D. Wyman and Clifton B. Kroeber (Madison 1958) 210, and Martin B. Fried, "The Sources, Composition, and Popularity of Mark Twain's *Roughing It*," unpublished Ph.D. dissertation (Chicago 1951) 16.
[8] Franklin R. Rogers, *The Pattern for Mark Twain's Roughing It: Letters from Nevada by Samuel and Orion Clemens, 1861–1862* (Berkeley 1961) 19–21.

shatter the illusions of a pious, genteel, and excessively sentimental mother. That is, the relationship between the fictive mother and son in these letters prefigures the Mr Twain-Mr Brown relationship of the Sandwich Islands letters.

No evidence exists to indicate clearly the details of Twain's first draft of *Roughing It*, but a logical deduction from the available evidence is that, after the difficulties encountered with the point of view in *The Innocents Abroad*, he had returned to the Mr Twain-Mr Brown conflict of the Sandwich Islands and *Alta Californian* letters, patterning his narrator after Mr Twain and his companion, renamed Bemis, after Mr Brown. In the finished text, the narrator's gullibility, revealed in his prevision of the journey, and his sentimentality, his predisposition to view things through the "mellow moonshine of romance," are indications of his kinship with Mr Twain and ultimately with Dr Syntax.[9] And certainly Bemis exhibits in his infrequent appearances most of the characteristics of Mr Brown not only when he climaxes the "noble sport" of buffalo hunting ignobly treed by the bull but also when he launches out on his own in Salt Lake City and experiments with a local concoction known as "valley tan" with predictable results. Such traces of the burlesque conventions in the finished text strongly suggest a more fully developed traveler-companion relationship in the first draft, that is, before the revision which Twain described to his brother.

Apparently, then, the *Gate City* letters taught Twain how he could dispense with such a character as Bemis and how he could link the contradictory points of view of a Mr Twain and a Mr Brown in the one character. As Professor Henry Nash Smith has demonstrated (p 212), in the prevision of the journey and in much of the subsequent text "the pronoun 'I' links two quite different personae: the tenderfoot setting out across the Plains, and the old-timer, the veteran, who has seen the elephant and now looks back upon his own callow days of inexperience." Sophisticated and sentimental at the outset, the narrator's romantic expectations are shattered by the experiences of his journey and residence in the mining districts of Nevada. Envisioned at first as a character analogous to Mr Twain, the narrator is transformed by his experiences into a character analogous to Mr Brown.

Such a manipulation of the point of view, in itself a relatively simple affair, has enormous consequences for the art of that fiction which strives to build the illusion of objective reality. Stendhal's contribution to the development of literary realism, according to Erich Auerbach, is the

---

[9] Rogers, *Mark Twain's Burlesque Patterns* 61–66.

technique of placing fictive characters in an externally real historical and social continuum: "Insofar as the serious realism of modern times," he declares, "cannot represent man otherwise than as embedded in a total reality, political, social, and economic, which is concrete and constantly evolving . . . Stendhal is its founder." [10] To the sort of time-perspective exploited by Stendhal, Twain added an internal time-perspective gained by the evolution of his narrator from tenderfoot to old-timer, an evolution which is implicit in the point of view from the very beginning of the narrative when, in introducing the tenderfoot's prevision of the journey, the old-timer comments, "I was young and ignorant." A great deal of the verisimilitude in the subsequent narrative derives from this manipulation of the point of view. By presenting the tenderfoot's prevision in a burlesque tone and coupling with it the old-timer's explicit disdain of his youthful folly, Twain predisposes the reader to a willing suspension of disbelief when the reader encounters the fictive reality which has transformed the tenderfoot into the old-timer and upon which the old-timer bases his judgment. As far as the reader is concerned, the technique contributes materially to the obscuring of the distinctions between the fictive world in which the narrator moves and the external reality of travel across the Plains and life in the silver-mining regions of Nevada in the early 1860s.

The internal time-perspective, the movement from youthful delusion to mature skepticism, is not the only important consequence of the change in point of view. The movement is one in space as well as in time, almost literally a journey along a road to reality, and the wisdom of the old-timer results not so much from the time elapsed since he started out on his journey as it does from his removal from one geographical region to another and his consequent initiation, as Professor Smith has noted, into a new society, the society of the mining regions (p 214–219). The shift in the point of view has produced a shift in the nature of the conflict which now becomes an internal one based on the differences between the mores of the East and those of the West. Bearing with him on his journey not only the heritage of his youth in the eastern United States but also highly erroneous concepts gleaned from his readings about the West, the tenderfoot must learn to adjust to the mores of the new society before he can become the old-timer. The insecurity, the humiliation, and occasionally the danger attendant upon actions performed and attitudes revealed while one is ignorant of the basic rules of the "curious new world" in which he finds himself are at the heart of the first thirty-three chapters, that is, to that point where the introduction

[10] *Mimesis: The Representation of Reality in Western Literature* (New York 1957) 408.

of a new tenderfoot, General Buncombe, signals the narrator's own emergence into the community of old-timers. One humorous illustration of this inner conflict is the narrator's encounter with the desperado Slade:

> The coffee ran out. At last it was reduced to one tincupful, and Slade was about to take it when he saw that my cup was empty. He politely offered to fill it, but although I wanted it, I politely declined. I was afraid he had not killed anybody that morning, and might be needing diversion. But still with firm politeness he insisted on filling my cup, and said I had traveled all night and better deserved it than he — and while he talked he placidly poured the fluid, to the last drop. I thanked him and drank it, but it gave me no comfort, for I could not feel sure that he would not be sorry, presently, that he had given it away, and proceed to kill me to distract his thoughts from the loss.

As a further consequence of the shift in point of view, Twain transformed burlesque into a remarkably effective fictive representation of the experience of those sensitive Americans whose adult lives spanned the Civil War years. With basic convictions, often excessively optimistic, formed in the pre-Civil War era, such Americans suffered a most intense disillusionment in the postwar era while at the same time they gained the sobered maturity of, say, the Walt Whitman of "Out of the Cradle Endlessly Rocking." Vernon L. Parrington was correct when, in opening his discussion of Mark Twain in the third volume of his *Main Currents,* he identified the narrator of *Roughing It* as the image of the post-Civil War American. Certainly Twain's old-timer is as powerful an image for this period as Cooper's Natty Bumppo is for the former. But Parrington was quite wrong when he chose the tenderfoot's brief spree in stock speculation to epitomize the American of the Gilded Age. The American whom Twain epitomized with the narrator of *Roughing It* is one who, nurtured in one culture, suddenly finds himself faced with the necessity of adjusting to another, or succumbing. One indication of the accuracy of Twain's image appears in the parallel between the narrator of *Roughing It* and the Henry Adams of *The Education.* What Twain achieved with the two personae merged in the pronoun "I," Adams achieved by writing his autobiography in the third person: the detachment and distance of the educated Adams from the Henry Adams who was undergoing the painful and seemingly fruitless education. Like Twain's old-timer, the Henry Adams of the twentieth century looks back with disdain upon what it pleased him to call his deluded "eighteenth-century youth," chronicles the events which produced the maturity, and reveals what is implicit in Twain's narrative, the loss as well as the gain of education. Although we can perceive it in the book, Twain did not make much of the point that the gaining of maturity necessarily involves a loss of that freedom from reality upon which the romantic imagination is based. The point is, nevertheless, implicit in the *Weekly Occidental* episode which occupies a rather prominent place toward the end of the adventures in Nevada. In this episode, the narrator and several fellow old-timers attempt to write a "sensation" novel in instalments for their literary weekly. But the narrator and his fellow novelists are totally unable to produce such flights of the imagination as those upon which the tenderfoot's preconception of the Far West had been based. Later, in *Old Times on the Mississippi*, Twain was more explicit. Commenting upon the results of the cub's education as a river pilot, he wrote,

> Now when I had mastered the language of this water and had come to know every trifling feature that bordered the great river as familiarly as I knew the letters of the alphabet, I had made a valuable acquisition. But I had lost something, too. I had lost something which could never be restored to me while I lived. All the grace, the beauty, the poetry, had gone out of the majestic river!

The hero which Twain thus developed differs somewhat from the Young Man from the Provinces, whom Professor Lionel Trilling discerned as the defining hero in "a great line of novels" running "through the nineteenth-century as . . . the very backbone of its fiction." Professor Trilling describes the Young Man as one who "need not come from the provinces in literal fact, his social class may constitute his province. But a provincial birth and rearing suggest the simplicity and the high hopes he begins with — he starts with a great demand upon life and a great wonder about its complexity and promise. He may be of good family but he must be poor. He is intelligent, or at least aware, but not at all shrewd in worldly matters. He must have acquired a certain amount of education, should have learned something about life from books, although not the truth." [11] Twain's hero differs primarily in the assurance which is his as a result of his illusions. Confident of his superiority, or at least of his equality, in ability, social station, and sophistication, he eagerly embarks upon a penetration into a strange society, only to be exposed by his very illusions in a series of experiences to the painful truth that he has been deluded, that he must discard his previous self-conception. The successful learning of this lesson, although it involves the loss of youthful ebullience, brings mature self-knowledge.

All this is to say that the conflict which Twain developed from the mutation of the burlesque conventions anticipates that of the international novel

---

[11] Lionel Trilling, "The Princess Casamassima," *The Liberal Imagination* (New York 1950) 61.

later developed by Henry James, which Professor Oscar Cargill has defined as a novel "in which a character, usually guided in his actions by the mores of one environment, is set down in another, where his learned reflexes are of no use to him, where he must employ all his individual resources to meet successive situations, and where he must intelligently accommodate himself to the new mores, or, in one way or another, be destroyed." [12] The anticipation suggests a relatively close bond between Twain and James. But the closeness is obscured by Professor Cargill's failure to stress in his definition two essential elements: the initial illusory self-conception which precipitates a course of action leading toward an anticipated conquest in the new society, and the self-discovery resulting from the disappointment of his hopes.

Twain took the comic view; James, the tragic, first in *The American*. In doing so James created a character, Christopher Newman, whose attitudes, background, and even physical appearance are close enough to those of Twain or his fictive counterparts in *The Innocents Abroad* and *Roughing It* to cause the reader to suspect a direct indebtedness. James, of course, gave to the theme perhaps its most embracing significance when almost as if he were retelling the story of Hawthorne's Miriam, he took another American innocent, Isabel Archer, along the road that led to Rome. "Rome was actual," Henry Adams discovered on the eve of the Civil War: to him Rome meant the first painful realization of the enchainment, the confinement of the romantic imagination, the anchoring of a soaring idealism to the hard and heavy facts of actuality. To Isabel, Rome finally signifies substantially the same thing. Envisioning happiness, at the outset of her European adventures, as dashing over a strange road in a coach and four on a dark night, so self-confident and assured of a special destiny that she refuses Lord Warburton with but little trepidation, she discovers herself in Rome married to Gilbert Osmond, confined to a "dark narrow alley with a blind wall at the end." Rome is indeed the actual for her when she turns away from Caspar Goodwood's impassioned embrace to follow the "very straight path" back to Osmond.

When we recall the differences between the two writers, the fact that James was impelled to express in his fiction a theme almost identical with Twain's attests to the accuracy and, one might almost say, the universality of the image of the American evoked by the mutation of the burlesque conventions in Twain's *Roughing It*.

---

[12] Oscar Cargill, "The First International Novel," *PMLA* LXXIII (Sept 1958) 419.

Postscript

Just as this volume was being compiled, the following

Bulletin article was received. It can serve as an interesting

postscript to the discussion. — ED.

Fact and Fiction in
Captain John Smith's *True Travels*

By Philip L. Barbour

FOR MORE THAN a century, a teapot tornado has whirled in so-called scholarly works about the general credibility of Captain John Smith's writings. Specifically, the "Pocahontas Incident" and Smith's adventures in Europe have been the butts of extensive experiments in debunking, although hints were thrown out by the Reverend Thomas Fuller as early as the middle 1600s that Smith was generally a liar — with Fuller making at least one misstatement himself.[1] But the Incident claimed attention first in this country and was the spring-board for Henry Adams' famous attack on Smith's veracity.[2] What that may have been about is treated in my biography of Smith, now in the press. The present study deals with Smith's early life only, as related in his *True Travels*.[3]

Although Fuller had long since written that the scene of Smith's adventures "is laid at such a distance, they are cheaper credited than confuted," it was two centuries and more before anyone seriously took up the task of impugning the *True Travels*. Suspect though they were to many, no one was equipped to attack the work directly until a Hungarian engineer and amateur historian named Lajos (Lewis) Kropf seized a blunderbuss and started shooting in all directions. After a preliminary shot in 1888, in 1890 he swept Smith's account from end to end, labeled the author an impostor and the book a "pseudo-historical romance," and put the stamp of historical falsity on the *True Travels*, at least so far as they dealt with Central Europe.[4] American historians swallowed the Kropf "exposé," generally with gusto, and without inquiring into Kropf's own reliability. Captain John Smith was all but discredited, especially among those who were not in a position to judge either Smith or Kropf. Indeed, the 1950s rolled around before modern

[1] Thomas Fuller, *The History of the Worthies of England* (new ed, 3 vols, London 1840) i 275–276.

[2] Henry Adams, "Captain John Smith," *North American Review*, civ (Jan 1867) 1–30.

[3] *The True Travels, Adventvres, and Observations of Captaine Iohn Smith, in Europe, Asia, Affrica, and America, from Anno Domini 1593 to 1629* (London, Printed by J. H. for Thomas Slater 1630). Several copies of the *True Travels* are in the Rare Book Division of The New York Public Library.

[4] Lewis L. Kropf, "Notes," *Notes and Queries*, 7th ser, ix (1890) 1–2, 41–43, 102–104, 161–162, 223–224, and 281–282.

research began to be applied, first by Bradford Smith and Dr Laura Polanyi Striker, and in short order by the present author.[5]

Basically, those who have let fly at the truth of the *True Travels* have completely lost sight of the conditions under which Smith "toured" Europe. To their way of thinking, obviously, the unwealthy farmer's boy from Lincolnshire who set out to seek adventure with an elementary-school education and $25 in his pocket [6] should have carried with him notebooks and pencils, spy-glasses, surveying instruments, and vocabularies at least of Latin, High German, Transylvanian Saxon, Hungarian, Turkish, Greek and Russian. These impedimenta he should have preserved through being thrown overboard by a "rabble of pilgrims," through the battles around Limbach and Stuhlweissenburg in Hungary, and through the siege of a fortress near Alba Iulia, Transylvania. He should have carried them also with him when he was wounded and taken prisoner by Tartars, kept them in Istanbul where he was a slave, and later used them to measure distances trudged over in chains and to note down names of villages passed en route. And finally he should have hauled this equipment with him across the Black Sea in a slave-galley to a Turkish timar up the River Don, kept it on the farm where he labored, and carefully packed it up for transportation across all of southern Russia when he murdered the slave-driver and escaped. Meanwhile, these modern realists feel, Smith should have learned enough Hungarian, Turkish, Greek and Russian to know what was going on and write down names accurately, and, when he got his passport from Zsigmond Báthory in 1603, he should have put that in a safe-deposit box while he went to fight Indians in America and pirates on the Atlantic, instead of taking it with him while he swam to safety through a storm near La Rochelle in 1615. Such appear to be the expectancies of some historians. Because Smith merely wrote things down from memory, years later, he is a liar.

More soberly, let us see what the facts of the case are. A little knowledge of geography and a bowing acquaintance with a few languages are required to find them. Then, to interpret them there is needed some familiarity with common human behavior and with the mentality of soldiers, sailors,

[5] See especially Bradford Smith, *Captain John Smith: His Life and Legend* (Philadelphia 1953), which includes Dr Striker's primary work; Laura Polanyi Striker, "The Hungarian Historian, Lewis L. Kropf, on Captain John Smith's *True Travels*," *Virginia Magazine of History and Biography* (herein after called *VMHB*) LXVI (1958) 22–43; and my two articles, "Captain John Smith's Route through Turkey and Russia," *William and Mary Quarterly*, 3rd ser, XIV (1957) 358–369, and "Captain John Smith's Observations on Life in Tartary," *VMHB*, LXVIII (1960) 271–283.

[6] He had 10 shillings; the valuation of $25 is merely to hint that he had little. No scientific valuation of a shilling in terms of modern purchasing power is possible.

explorers, and gentlemen of the gaudy days of James I of Great Britain, France and Ireland. Armed with such of these requirements as we can muster, here is the story.

No original manuscript of the *True Travels* exists today. Fortunately, however, two printed editions of the bulk of the work, if not all of it, are available. The earlier, and briefer, of these was written sometime between 1622 and 1625 and included in Samuel Purchas's *Hakluytus Posthumus*.[7] It forms Chapter XI of Part I, Book 8, and bears the title: *The Travels and Adventures of Captaine John Smith in divers parts of the world, begun about the yeere 1596.* The other edition, registered for publication as a separate little volume in 1629, appeared in 1630 with the title: *The True Travels, Adventures, and Observations of Captaine John Smith, in Europe, Asia, Affrica, and America, from Anno Domini 1593 to 1629.* Small as the volume is, only about two thirds of it are taken up with Smith's *Adventures*, while the balance is a continuation of Smith's earlier *Generall Historie of Virginia*. Only the autobiographical part concerns us here, and that is almost identical (outside of a number of variant spellings) with the version printed by Purchas. This study is based on the version of 1629.

In all, the first two-thirds of the *True Travels* contain about five hundred names of places and people, and peoples.[8] Allowing for the vagaries of early seventeenth-century spelling, it can be said that four-fifths of these names are readily recognizable today, all vouched for by sources quite independent of John Smith. The remaining hundred or so are less certain, or far from certain, and are a proper subject for investigation.

Smith's life story starts off in good style with two misprints in the second sentence: *Crudley* for *Cuerdley* (Lancashire), and *Rickand* for *Rickard* (or *Riccard*), the name of his mother's family.[9] Since we have that warning, there is no reason to be puzzled, a page or so later, by such names as *Ripweth* (for *Rippeth* or *Redpath*, in Berwickshire) and *Broxmoth* (for *Broxmouth*, in East Lothian). Yet the notable editor of Smith's *Works*, Edward Arber, was unable to locate these places.[10]

Theadora Polaloga, stated a few lines below to have taught Smith to ride and to joust, could be called more puzzling, but a little inquiry will soon reveal that he was undoubtedly Theodore Paleologue, a collateral descend-

[7] Samuel Purchas, *Hakluytus Posthumus, or Purchas His Pilgrimes* (4 vols, London 1625; reprinted in 20 vols, Glasgow 1905–1907).

[8] Including a certain amount of evident duplication, the total is 509.

[9] *Capt. John Smith: Works*, ed Edward Arber (The English Scholar's Library, Birmingham 1884), p 821.

[10] *Works*, p xxv.

ant from the last East Roman Emperor who was killed defending his capital from the Turks in 1453. Theodore, born in Pesaro, Italy, went to England as a hired assassin for the Republic of Lucca, failed to carry out his mission, obtained employment from the Earl of Lincoln, married one Mary Balls at the Earl's Tattershall castle on May 1 1600, and died in Saltash, Cornwall, January 21 1636.[11]

Smith had been in France and the Netherlands before meeting Paleologue, and he returned to the latter sometime in 1600, apparently after the battle of Nieuport, fought on June 22 (or July 2, according to the new calendar).[12] He undoubtedly wanted to see service again, but soldiering died down rapidly after Nieuport, and there was little if any recruiting. Somewhere he picked up "four French Gallants," and between them a plan was evolved to go fight the Turks, who had renewed their attacks on Hungary in 1593. Smith reports that he was cheated by the "gallants," but the interesting side of this adventure consists in the names he records.

One of the quartet was a "great Lord" named Depreau, and his companions were "three young citizens: Cursell, La Nelie, and Monferrat." Lanelly (or Lannilis) and Montferrat are recognizable as names, nothing more. DePreau, on the other hand, is intriguing. That was the name used in Scotland by the French Ambassador to James VI in 1586, whose real name was M. D'Esneval, sieur de Courcelles. It was also the name of the almoner of Mary, Queen of Scots. Somehow, the DePreau and Courcelles of Scottish history must be connected with Smith's Lord Depreau and citizen Cursell.[13]

It would be idle to list all the correspondences in name between the petty nobility Smith met in northern France and the personal- or place-names recorded in books and on maps. Smith's spelling is his own, usually, but the places can easily be found — the first group near "Mortaigne," as Smith spells Mortain, Normandy. In Brittany Smith's "Earl of Ployer" and his brothers "Viscount Poomory" and "Baron d'Mercy" were young Amaury II Goyon (or Gouyon), Comte de Plouër and his eldest brothers, who would have been known by the second and third family titles, Vicomte de Tonquedec

[11] Information from an unpublished monograph by Canon John H. Adams, Landulph Rectory, Saltash, Cornwall, *Theodore Paleologus, "The Greek Prince of Cornwall,"* a copy of which was lent me by the author. I take this opportunity to express my thanks.

[12] *Battle of Nieuport, 1600;* Shakespeare Association Facsimile No 9 (London 1935).

[13] On the French Ambassador, see *Extract from the Despatches of M. Courcelles . . .* , ed Robert Bell, Bannatyne Club, vol xxii (Edinburgh 1828); *Letters of Mary, Queen of Scots,* ed Agnes Strickland (2 vols, London 1843), ii 171, 184, 201, 236, 243, and 283; and various references in the *Calendar of State Papers, Scotland* ix 1586–1588 (see Index).

et de Pommerith, and Baron de Marcé. Smith visited "their own fair Castle of Tuncadeck."[14]

Smith's "Master Curzianvere" (or Currianver), who befriended him from the outset, alone remains totally unidentifiable among these French friends. Clearly, the extraordinary historians of the nineteenth century (and later!) could have taken the trouble to look into these matters before passing judgment. They are at fault, not John Smith.

On leaving France, however, Smith comes up with a detail which is puzzling indeed. He took ship for Italy, which was the safest and quickest way to get there in those days, but ran into foul weather and fouler companions. He was taken for a heretic and a pirate, and fair weather would never come so long as he was aboard. So they pitched him over the side, near "the little Isle of S. Mary, against Neice in Savoy," which was uninhabited but for cattle and goats.

There is nothing remotely resembling an island near Nice today, although Port Lympia by the Old Town was nothing but a swampy bay in 1600, and some unrecorded island may have existed. But unless Smith is referring to another St Mary's island, not near Nice, there is no clue to the name. It is after all unimportant, for no one has called Smith a liar on account of the little Isle of Saint Mary.[15]

After a wet night in the company of goats that did not care whether he was a heretic or not, Smith was picked up by a Captain La Roche, a Protestant of St-Malo, and taken on a tour of the Mediterranean aboard a French trading-ship. His route is clear, and there are no questions, although it is proper to note that Smith's *Cape Rosata* is not the Rosetta mouth of the Nile, but Cape Ras-et-Tin, in Cyrenaica, in the region famous in 1941–1942 for Rommel and his Afrika-Korps. The winter passed, and sometime in the summer of 1601 Smith reached Graz in southern Austria. He was at last ready to fight the Turks.

Smith apparently had acquired some knowledge of French, and with the aid of school-Latin he picked up a little Italian. His references to names in those languages are generally not difficult to interpret. In Austria, on the

14 Investigation of the identity of Smith's "Earl of Ployer" was begun by Bradford Smith as stated in his "Notes," *VMHB* LXII (1954) 348–349. The clue given there was followed by me, first in the Map Division, The New York Public Library, beginning with Pierre A. Girault de Saint Fargeau, *Dictionnaire Géographique . . . de toutes les communes de la France* (Paris 1844), followed by a number of other works available there. Final tracking down was completed in the Reference Department of The New York Public Library, in the British Museum, and on the spot in France (Château de Plouër, and in the Municipal Archives at Rennes).

15 On Port Lympia's history, see Robert Latouche, *Histoire de Nice* (2 vols, Nice 1951–1954) I 45.

other hand, he made his first acquaintance with German, and also with the Central European Tower of Babel. The common soldiers might be of almost any nationality. The officers spoke German or French or Italian, when they were not Hungarians, but the peasants in the countryside spoke nothing but Hungarian, or some Slavic language. In addition the Germans themselves did not always speak High German, but often had a pronunciation which converted Wagensberg to Boginsperk, for example. Since Smith did not know how to spell the names he heard, he wrote them down as best he could (in some cases, years later), and not according to some phonetic system. This has thrown many scholars off the track, particularly because few of the names bear any superficial resemblance to names known from history books.

Smith opens his account by saying that an Englishman and an Irish Jesuit in Graz, to whom he seems to have had letters, made him acquainted with "many brave Gentlemen," especially one known as *Lord Ebersbaught*. Ebersbaught in turn presented Smith to *Baron Kisell*, an artillery officer, and Kisell passed him on to "a worthy Colonel, the Earl of Meldritch." Meldritch accepted Smith in his regiment, and soon they were off to the war.

These names could easily have remained mysteries had not Ebersbaught "preferred" Smith to Kisell, for Kisell is the only one of the three whose name is not distorted almost out of recognition. History shows that Hans Jakob Khissl was Court War Counselor of the Archduke Ferdinand and Lieutenant Colonel of the Arsenal (viz, the artillery).[16] The succession of presentations shows that Khissl was a friend of both Ebersbaught and Meldritch. This supplies the clue.

The petty nobility of the Krain, the region just south of Graz, included the Khissls and a family named Eibiswald (pronounced roughly Ee-bass-bawlt — surely Smith's Ebersbaught), representatives of both of which sat in the local diet or parliament. With them sat also the Frangipani (Frankopan family), Counts of Modrusch. Modrusch was pronounced Mödritsch. Smith's Meldritch is almost unquestionably a member of this family.[17]

Following the same clue, it becomes clear that many of the Christians involved in the battles described by Smith came from the same regional

[16] See J. Franz Pichler's "Captain John Smith in the Light of Styrian Sources," *VMHB* LXV (1957) 332–354, with the results of what may be called preliminary investigation. In the summer of 1960, with the aid of Dr Pichler and sources too numerous to mention here, I was able to reconstruct some of the intricate family connections while searching in the Archives at Graz.

[17] On Modrusch / Mödritsch, I am particularly indebted to Dr F. von Metnitz, Sauerlach, Oberbayern, and Dr Hans Sokoll, Heraldisch-Genealogische Gesellschaft "Adler," Vienna, for several letters to me (in early 1961), clarifying a number of details, and circumstantially proving the identity Modrusch = Meldritch.

nobility, and can therefore be identified with some degree of certainty. Smith's *Culnits,* for instance, was undoubtedly a Kollonitsch, a "new" family which by intermarrying with the Eibiswalds succeeded to the arms and titles of the extinct Kollnitz family, which in turn had provided a marital link between the Khissls and the Eibiswalds. (Hans Jakob Khissl's brother married Katharina von Kollnitz. Katharina's aunt married Veit Eibiswald. Veit's niece married Daniel zu Kollonitsch, making the latter a sort of cousin.) On the other side of the Eibiswald family, Georg Khissl's wife was related by marriage to Katharina von Eibiswald, who married a Wagen von Wagensberg. Felician Wagen von Wagensberg, who was very likely Smith's *Vahan,* was another of these local nobles involved in the Turkish wars of the time.[18] Thanks to Smith's *Kisell* and *Vahan,* the "unidentifiable" names become merely a typical tangle of local "blue-blood" relationships.

As for the Transylvanian officers with whom Smith was associated in 1602, every one of these can be referred with certainty to place-names, the great bulk of which are to be found on contemporary maps. In many cases Smith may have refreshed his memory with the aid of such maps. But the names of the Turkish officers are so conspicuously non-Turkish for the most part that they seem added merely to give color to the story. Here we evidently have an element of fiction, not to be deplored as unhistorical, but accepted as contributing to the vividness of Smith's narrative.

For example, that Smith fought three duels can hardly be doubted. That he heard the names, or at least descriptive epithets, of his opponents and that they sounded most "exotic" to his Lincolnshire ears is highly probable. But that he should recall such names with the accuracy of an orientalist through the vicissitudes of twenty years would be expecting a great deal of him. It is therefore well-nigh useless to attempt to guess what *Turbashaw, Grualgo,* and *Bonny Mulgro* represent in the original language. (Turbashaw may of course be merely *Türk bashi,* "a Turkish captain.")

Smith's identification of Turks encountered in the field is more fictional. In a few instances he surely got the names from Richard Knolles' *Turkish History,* but the bulk of them are typical English or Latin forms of Turkish or Arabic names which Smith could hardly have heard on the spot.[19] This is the sense in which "fictional" is used for such names as: Aladin, Amaroz, and Zizimus "Bashaws." *Bogall Bashaw* may be a descriptive title distorted

[18] Information from personal communications to me, supplemented by: *Steiermärkisches Wappen-Buch von Zacharias Bartsch 1567* . . . , ed Josef von Zahn and Alfred Ritter Anthony von Siegenfeld (Graz and Leipzig 1893); Dr Hans Kloepfer, *Eibiswald* (Graz / Vienna / Leipzig 1933); Johann Weichard, *Die Ehre des Herzogthums Krain* (Ljubljana / Nuremberg 1689); and other sources largely unavailable outside Austria.

[19] See Richard Knolles, *The Turkish History* . . . (6th ed, 3 vols, London 1687–1700).

from *bakkal*, "spice merchant," plus *bashi*, "chief"; but generally none of these captains and petty officials were *pashas*, as Smith's spelling would indicate. *Assan* (Hasan) and *Amaroz* (Murad) *Bashaw*, probably the only exceptions, were, respectively, the general in command of the army and the pasha of Buda.[20] (Pest, lacking a fortress, had virtually ceased to exist.)

When it came to the names of places, rather than people, Smith for the most part relied on his own memory and his flair for geography. But because he spelled these names his own way much good paper and ink has been wasted in idle speculation. Smith's *Olumpagh* (or *Olimpach*), where he won his captaincy, is obviously Limbach, but because there are several Limbachs it has been the subject of needless discussion. On the basis of location, terrain, and history, it can only be the place called Lendava, Yugoslavia, today — the "Lower Limbach" which suffered a recorded attack in 1601, the year when Smith was there. The prefixed *O-* is quite simply explained: the Latin name was Olimacum, and "the 'o' was cut off by barbarians."[21] Smith's pedantic friend Samuel Purchas probably restored the *O-* after Smith got back to London, but Smith insisted on keeping the rest of the word as he had heard it: O-Limbach, not Olimacum. The typesetters did the rest.

The next geographical problem, after passages of remarkable clarity, is offered by Smith's "Plaines of Girke." The site was not far from Stuhlweissenburg (Hungarian Székesfehérvár), and one or two scholars pounced on Girke, a name occurring on de Bry's map of Hungary, as the place. Girke, however, represents the Hungarian village of Györköny (pronounced roughly like "jerkin"), nearly 50 miles south of Stuhlweissenburg. This location does not fit in with Smith's description of what happened. His regiment set out, he says, to meet a Turkish army under General Hasan Pasha

---

[20] The suggestion regarding Bogall Bashaw is from Dr Franz Babinger (personal letter dated Oct 3 1960). The distinction between Bashaw = pasha (a title of high rank) and Bashaw = bashi ("head," such as a captain) was pointed out to me by Professor Tibor Halasi-Kun of Columbia University, in conversations late in 1960. John Smith did not distinguish between them any more than the bulk of writers. Hasan Pasha is well-known in history, but an interesting detail appears in connection with Smith's "Amaroz," or Murad, Pasha. According to Joseph von Hammer-Purgstall's *Geschichte des Osmanischen Reiches* (10 vols, Pest 1827–1835) iv 314, the correct name of the Pasha of Buda was Mankirkouschi Mohammed, and it was the Hungarian historian Nikolaus Istvanffi who mis-named him Murad in his *Historiarum de Rebus Ungaricis Libri IV* (Cologne 1622). Smith must have picked the name up from some German or Hungarian colleague at Stuhlweissenburg itself, but it seems strange that the Christians did not know the Pasha's name.

[21] See Wolfgang Lazius, *Reipublicae Romanae in Exteris Provinciis . . . Libri duodecim* (Frankfurt am Main 1598), p 968–969. Smith's Knousbruck (or Konbrucke) and Hysnaburg (or Eysnaburg), mentioned in connection with Olumpagh, remain obscure. I believe the latter to be somehow derived from Hosszúfalu—a mere guess—while Knousbruck requires further study.

Buda is in upper right, "Stulweissenburg" center. Detail, de Bry's map of Hungary
(see footnote 22, p 110).

and the Pasha of Buda which was advancing from the direction of Buda, presumably; i e, from the northeast, not from the south.

Turkish histories of the campaign identify the place. The Ottoman army met the Christians "under the walls of Stuhlweissenburg" in Tscharka Pass, some fifteen miles away near Lake Velencse. The date was October 15 1601, according to the Gregorian calendar. Tscharka then is Smith's Girke, but we may suspect that Smith took his spelling from de Bry's map. He could not find the "right" place in any geography.[22]

What happened for the next four months Smith does not report. Probably the armies were in winter-quarters. Before spring, however, Smith's regiment was again on the move, this time to try to bring order in chaotic Transylvania. The historical details can be found in Smith's *True Travels*, but it is important for the investigation of his place-names to know that he and his fellow-soldiers could have entered that principality only from the northwest. The west and the south were in the hands of the Turks.

Smith writes, obscurely, that his commander "made many incursions into the land of Zarkam [Zarkain], among those rocky mountains," and this has been interpreted as referring to Sárkány (Sercaia).[23] But again we have an interpretation which ignores what was going on. The Imperial General for the Transylvanian campaign, Giorgio Basta, was occupied in February 1602 in the region between Bistritz and Klausenburg, as they were then generally called, while his opponent, Prince Zsigmond Báthory, was at Kronstadt (Brassó), 200 or so miles to the south, by roads passable in the winter, Sarkany was only 30 miles from Kronstadt, and for that reason can hardly have been Smith's Zarkain. It would appear far more likely that Zarkain refers to the region around Markt Schelken, half way to Kronstadt and in the mountains, as described by John Smith.

Markt Schelken, the largest of three "Schelkens," is 50 miles east of Alba Iulia, capital of Transylvania, which can be said definitely to have been iden-

---

[22] See Theodor de Bry's *Vetvstissimi potentissimiqve Hvngariae Regni . . . 1596*, a map in his *Pannoniae Historia Chronologica*, Frankfurt am Main 1596, (Rare Book Division, NYPL; photostat in Map Division). I am grateful to the Map Division Chief, Mr Gerard L. Alexander, and his staff for their tireless cooperation in producing the huge number of maps, old and modern, general and detailed, which had to be studied in connection with John Smith's *True Travels*. The task was not lightened by the difficult toponymy of Hungary and Transylvania, where almost every town, village, river and hill has a German as well as a Hungarian name, and many boast Rumanian or Slavic names to boot — not to mention Latin names for the larger cities. I have generally used the German names here, to avoid confusion, since these correspond with the names Smith used.

[23] The map of Transylvania by Ioannes Sambucus (No. 78, in Abraham Ortelius's *Theatrum Orbis Terrarum* [Antwerp 1579]) equates Zarkam with Schirkingen, some miles above Fogaras in southern Transylvania. Dr Striker (see footnote 5) identifies it with Sárkány, which is evidently the same place.

tified as the "Urbs Regalis" mentioned in Smith's *True Travels*. Here Smith participated in the siege of a nameless fortified "Cittie," before whose walls he fought the three duels mentioned above. And it was at Alba Iulia, known in German as Weissenburg, that John Smith was granted *Three Turks Heads* for use on his shield by "his Prince," Zsigmond Báthory.[24]

The remaining place-names reported by Smith for Transylvania and Walachia are immediately recognizable, with the exception of Raza. This may be guessed, on geographic and phonetic grounds, to be Brezoiu, Rumania, but it must remain a guess until evidence is found at least that the place existed in 1602. It is worth noting only, with some amusement, that Smith calls the valley in which he fought his last fight in Europe "Veristhorne," while referring to the neighboring "mountain of Rottenton." Vöröstorony is the Hungarian name for Red Tower, which is Rothenturm in German.

Smith's personal names, on the other hand, are largely perplexing. His pen runs along so glowingly as he describes the greatest battle of his career that we may suspect him of picking names at random to color an already colorful account. Nevertheless it is only his opponents who appear fanciful — not his associates — and even they bear evidence of being derived from some actual name. It cannot be said that they are proven inventions.

At the battle of Red Tower Pass Smith was taken prisoner, to be sold later as a slave. The date seems to have been November 18 1602. Many months passed before he escaped, during which he traveled to Istanbul and to Varna, across the Black Sea and up the Don, and through the no-man's land of southern Russia which then was called the *Dikoye Polye* — the Wilderness — to an outpost of the Muscovite Empire. Many "fanciful" names are found in this part of the *True Travels*, some of which, for all their odd appearance, are genuine, but others must have been added, years after, in London.

Smith calls his mistress "the young Charatza Tragabigzanda," or Trabigzanda, which is modern Greek for "girl from Trebizond." He was sold in Axiopolis, which is recorded, but later was marched "from Constantinople, by Sander, Screwe, Panassa, Musa, Lastilla, to Varna, an ancient Citie upon the Blacke Sea." The first four names are a puzzle, a clue to which may be found in Lastilla — a place-name recorded in many maps of Smith's time. If Smith ran across Lastilla in Samuel Purchas's study while trying to estab-

24 Smith refers to "Esenberg," which must be Weissenburg (Alba Iulia), later called Karlsburg. Zsigmond Báthory is known to have arrived there by April 1 1602 (Roderich Gooss, ed, *Österreichische Staatsvorträge: Fürstentum Siebenbürgen*, Kommission für neuere Geschichte Österreichs, Veröffentlichungen, IX [Vienna 1911] 273).

lish his route, Purchas may be suspected of giving Smith the names Panassa (the classical River Panyssus) and Musa (Moesia) as well. *Screwe* then becomes obvious as a misprint for Serawe, a current spelling of Turkish *seray*, and *by Sander* may be taken as a garbled form of Byzantium, a name for Constantinople which apparently escaped John Smith's ears.[25]

The river Smith calls Bruapo or Bruago, on the other hand, seems almost certainly to have been inspired by Smith's Welsh engraver and friend, Robert Vaughan, who jokingly translated "Rat Isle" (Ile de Ré) into Welsh for Smith's "Map of Ould Virginia" — Ynys Llygod. Near the Ile de Ré was a famous salt-market on a broad river, named Brouage. When Smith was looking for a name for *his* broad river, Vaughan could well have come up with Brouage, deliberately or accidentally transformed into Bruago. (The *o* and the *e* were much alike in the handwriting of the day.) But even more probably the same Welsh artist inspired Smith with the name Cambria (or Cambia) for the nameless part of Tartary through which Smith said he had passed. Meanwhile Purchas had probably suggested Nalbrits and Aecopolis to Smith as names for the two forts he had visited. Both of these names date back to Claudius Ptolemy, the famous geographer.[26] They appeared on maps in the sixteenth century, although nobody knew exactly where they had been. Nor was Smith sure where he had been.

After leaving "Aecopolis," which was very likely one of the two Muscovite outposts of Valuiki and Izyum, Smith was able to learn more about where he was. From there on every place he mentions can be identified with certainty, or at least with a very high degree of probability. "Zumalacke," for instance, "by" which he went to "Caragnaw" (Chernava), is fairly obviously the *Izyumskii Shlyakh*, the beaten path that served as a road from Moscow due south to the borders of the Crimean Khanate. Similarly his "Castragan" is the road (or track) *k Astrakhani*, "towards Astrakhan." His "Duzihell" is taken from a direction in Russian: *do Zvyahelya*, "to [as far as] Zvyahel"; and so on. Only once does he substitute his imagination for his memory, where he apparently felt that he must name a lady who befriended him when he still wore the chains of a Turkish slave. So he named the wife of the Governor of "Aecopolis" Callamata — we imagine — after the southern Greek

---

[25] This will correct the suggestions to be found in my article on Smith's route in the *William and Mary Quarterly* (see footnote 5). While the explanation is still hypothetical, there are other hints that the passage may be tentatively "restored" to read: "from Constantinople (Byzantium), by the Old Seray at Adrianople, along the Panyssus River through Moesia, to Lastilla and Varna, an ancient city on the Black Sea."

[26] See, for example, Navaris and Exapolis in the Bertius ed of Claudius Ptolemy, *Theatri Geographiae veteris* (Amsterdam 1618), Europae Tabula octava.

port of Kalamata, where it is possible that Captain La Roche's ship took refuge in a storm three years before.

Large portions of the rest of Smith's *True Travels* are made up of quotations from the writings of others. It is therefore necessary to add only one detail. Smith tells a story of a watchmaker named Henry Archer, his servant

Engraving by Martin Droeshout, in John Smith's *True Travels*, 1630.   *Rare Book Division*

John Bull, and a lion-cub that was given to Archer in Morocco. Although no confirmation of Smith's story has yet been found, there is no question about the existence of Archer and Bull. Master Henry Archer was elected one of the two first wardens of the Company of Clockmakers of London when it was incorporated in 1631, and John Bull was one of those who joined him in subscribing to the Charter.[27]

[27] See Samuel Elliott Atkins and William Henry Overall, *Some Account of the Worshipful Company of Clockmakers of the City of London* (London 1881) p 11, 20, and elsewhere.

When all is said and done, then, Smith's *True Travels* can be called a factual work, so far as it has been possible to verify it, or to locate pertinent information. The following summary will bear this out:

Names clearly recorded on contemporary maps or in contemporary books	45
The same, but distorted by Smith	16
Known surnames, but without individual mention independent of Smith	4
Evidently distorted names, but probably factual	6
Apparently factual, but not identified	8
Added in London, from books and maps	8
Added in London in connection with Smith's passport	6
Fictional, until proven otherwise	11
TOTAL	104

Since the foregoing includes all names not immediately recognizable, the percentage of "fictional" names in the *True Travels* is small for the entire work — eleven which are gratuitously added and fourteen which apparently resulted from consultation with Purchas or Vaughan, or both. These twenty-five names amount to 4.9% of all names.[28]

This handful of invented or borrowed details adds spice to the story. The age demanded such vividness. Romance was not yet totally divorced from History, and History itself was Melodrama. With the royal favorite Buckingham murdered in 1628, King Charles took the first step that would lead him, too, to violent death. Parliament was dissolved in anger, in March 1629 — not to reconvene for eleven years. On the following August 29, John Smith's *True Travels* was entered for publication at Stationers' Hall, London.

[28] The restudy of Smith's route from Constantinople to Varna, undertaken since the publication of my article in the *Bulletin of The New York Public Library* LXVII (1963), 517–528, has affected the text above (p 111–112) and has changed the table and the percentage of "fictional" names slightly. Such minor alterations are to be expected from time to time, until some accident provides full clarification of all questionable names.

Index

Adams, Henry 96 98 101
Addison, Joseph 54 62 70
Albani, Allesandro, Cardinal 39
Albani, Francesco 76
Alexander, Gerard L 110
Alta Californian 92 94
Amidas, Philip 24
Anacharsis 45
Apollonius Rhodius 55
Arber, Edward 103
Archer, Henry 112–113
Arnold, Matthew 52
Atkins, Samuel Elliot 113
Auerbach, Erich 94

Babin, Jacques Paul 34 37
Babinger, Franz Carl Heinrich 108
Bacon, Francis 58
Balls, Mary 104
Barbauld, Mrs Anna Letitia 53
Barlowe, Arthur 24
Barthélémy, Jean Jacques 31 35 40 45–46
Bárthory, Zsigmond 110–111
Basingstoke, John 34
Basta, Giorgio 110
Beckford, William 55–56
Bell, Robert 104
Bentley, Richard 43–44
Berry, Duchesse de 51
Bertrand, Louis 31
Best, George 17 19 21
Beyle, Marie Henri (*pseudonym* De Stendhal) 94–95
Bigges, Walter 20
Bikélas, Demetrius 31
Bliss, Elisha 85
Bonny Mulgro 107
Borinski, Karl 31
Boswell, James 54 56 59 65
Bowra, Sir Cecil Maurice 28
Brand, Charles Peter 69 81
Bray, René 31
Brereton, John 24
Brown, Edward 34
Brown, Wallace Cable 49
Browne, John Ross 90
Bruce, Thomas, seventh Earl of Elgin 43 46–48
Bry, Theodor de 108 110
Brydone, Patrick 7–8 53–63 65–67
Buckingham, Duke of *See* Villiers
Bull, John 112–113
Burke, Edmund 57–58 62
Burnett, James, Lord Monboddo 53
Burrough, Sir John 16 18

Burton, Sir Richard Francis 89
Butler, Eliza Mirian 31
Byron, George Noel Gordon 8 32 47–50 69–73 79–83

Calderon de la Barca, Pedro 80
Candish, Master 22
Cantemir, Demetrius 49
Cargill, Oscar 98
Carlyle, Joseph Dacre 47
Carlyle, Thomas 46
Carracci family 76
Carrey, Jacques 35
Caulfield, James 38
Cavendish, Thomas 18 22
Cervantes Saavedra, Miguel de 87
Chambers, Sir William 42
Champion, Anthony 86
Chandler, Richard 42
Charles I 113
Charles II 36
Chesterfield, Earl of *See* Stanhope
Chishull, Edmund 37
City Gate, Keokuk 93
Clarke, Edward Daniel 37
Clarke, Martin Lowther 46
Clemens, Orion 93
Clemens, Samuel Langhorne (*pseudonym* Mark Twain) 85 90–98
Clodius 63
Coleridge, Samuel Taylor 62
Collins, William 57
Combe, William 86–88
Cook, James 22 53
Cooper, James Fenimore 96
Corregio, Antonio Allegri da 76
Coryate, Thomas 7
Courcelles, M D'Esneval, sieur de 104
Crabbe, George 86
Culnits, ——— 107
Cumberland, George 86
Cursell, ——— 104
Curzianvere (Currianver), Master 105
Curzon, Robert, Baron Zouche 89
Cushing, John D 67
Cust, Sir Lionel Henry 39
Cyrus 45

Daiches, David 28
Dalton, Richard 38
Dalzel, Andrew 43
Daniello, Bernardino 27
David, Jacques Louis 46
Davis, John 24
Dawkins, James 40